The Open Door

GERD THEISSEN

The Open Door

Variations on Biblical Themes

Translated by John Bowden

FORTRESS PRESS · **MINNEAPOLIS**

THE OPEN DOOR
Variations on Biblical Themes

First Fortress Press edition published 1991.

Translated by John Bowden from *Die Offene Tür: Biblische Variationen zu Predigttexten*, published 1991 by Christian Kaiser Verlag, Munich, © Christian Kaiser Verlag 1990.

Translation © John Bowden 1991.

Phototypeset by Intype, London, and printed in Great Britain by Billing & Sons Ltd, Worcester

Library of Congress Cataloging-in-Publication Data
Theissen. Gerd.
    [Offene Tür. English]
    The open door: variations on biblical themes/Gerd Theissen:
translated by John Bowden. — 1st Fortress Press ed.
        p.   cm.
    Translation of: Die offene Tür.
    ISBN 0-8006-2561-7
    1. Bible. N.T.—Sermons. 2. Germany—Social conditions—20th
century—Sermons. 3. Sermons, English. 4. Sermons, German.
5. Evangelische Landeskirche in Baden—Sermons. 6. United churches—
Germany—Sermons. I. Title.
BS2344.2.T4813   1991
252'.041—dc20
                                                                91-3143
                                                                    CIP

                                                        AF   1-2561

96 95 94 93 92 91   1 2 3 4 5 6 7 8 9 10

For my parents and family

84963

Contents

Contents

Preface

The sermons and meditations collected here were written in Copenhagen and Heidelberg between 1979 and 1989. Most of them were given to the congregation of the Peterskirche in the University of Heidelberg.

These sermons are 'variations on biblical themes' which interpret the Bible by retelling the text, adapting themes, changing perspectives or challenging ways in which the Bible is understood. Someone who heard them described them as 'reflective sermons'. In fact they are intended to prompt reflection by varying and elaborating on biblical images and narratives.

The variation form is bound up with my conviction that the images and narratives of the Bible have several dimensions. They illuminate existential, social and universal situations in life and turn them into a 'sign language' for God. Images and narratives have the advantage of being able to illuminate different contexts like lights, whereas the more precise abstract notions are, the more they are limited to particular spheres.

At many points the reader will detect a particular view of the preacher's task. Every living being is involved in an unconscious interaction with the overall system of reality. This interaction becomes conscious only in human beings – and takes its most developed form in the undertaking of a dialogue with God. To be a preacher means to prompt, illuminate, change this dialogue by redefining it in terms of that dialogue which came to be recorded in the Bible. Preachers have achieved their aim where the biblical text makes it possible to engage in dialogue with God, so that men and women can understand their lives as an answer to God's call – in all spheres of life: in personal, political and universal contexts.

Here preachers face tasks which seem to be insoluble: they have to transform what had meaning in the past into motivation for thought and action in the present. They have to give their personal experiences a generally valid form so as to become representatives of the community. They have to put the historical events of a year in contexts which point far beyond that year. In other words, they have to bring historical traditions, personal experience and contemporary history into dialogue with an ultimate reality, knowing full well that they cannot produce this dialogue. Its success is beyond their control. And it is good that that should be so, for every sermon intervenes in the most intimate dialogue which people have with themselves (and with God). Sermons touch a sphere which is vulnerable and should be protected from the attacks of other people. Preaching would be an intolerably indiscreet business did we not know that whether or not we reach this most intimate sphere is not up to us.

I have lightly revised all the sermons for publication, reducing the redundancy which is needed in spoken texts without losing the oral character of the sermons. In addition, I have added notes at the end of the book which indicate some sources and explain allusions and references to contemporary events. The sermons can be understood without the notes, but the detailed historical background of some of the passing allusions may perhaps be of interest to readers.

I am grateful to David Trobisch for his critical reading of the manuscript, to Hubert Meisinger for reading the proofs, to Bernd Raebel for collecting information for the notes, and to Wega Schmidt-Thomee and Helga Wolf for producing the manuscript. I am also grateful to those who heard the sermons in the congregation of the Peterskirche, above all to my wife.

My parents and family were not able to hear any of these sermons. That is why I have dedicated this written version to them. It is also in memory of those members of my family who have died: Else, Christoph and Hartmut Theissen.

Heidelberg, February 1990

For the English translation, the biblical texts and quotations have been taken from the New International Version.

Cain and Abel
A murder trial revisited

—

(Genesis 4.1-16)

Adam lay with his wife Eve, and she became pregnant and gave birth to Cain. She said, 'With the help of the Lord I have brought forth a man.' Later she gave birth to his brother Abel. Now Abel kept flocks, and Cain worked the soil. In the course of time Cain brought some of the fruits of the soil as an offering to the Lord. But Abel brought fat portions from some of the firstborn of his flock. The Lord looked with favour on Abel and his offering, but on Cain and his offering he did not look with favour. So Cain was very angry, and his face was downcast. Then the Lord said to Cain, 'Why are you angry? Why is your face downcast? If you do what is right, will you not be accepted? But if you do not do what is right, sin is crouching at your door; it desires to have you, but you must master it.' Now Cain said to his brother Abel, 'Let's go out to the field.' And while they were in the field, Cain attacked his brother Abel and killed him. Then the Lord said to Cain, 'Where is your brother Abel?' 'I don't know,' he replied, 'Am I my brother's keeper?' The Lord said, 'What have you done? Listen! Your brother's blood cries out to me from the ground. Now you are under a curse and driven from the ground, which opened its mouth to receive your brother's blood from your hand. When you work the ground, it will no longer yield its crops for you. You will be a restless wanderer on the earth.' Cain said to the Lord, 'My punishment is more than I can bear. Today you are driving me from the land, and I will be hidden from your presence; I will be a restless wanderer on the earth, and whoever finds me will kill me.' But the Lord said to him, 'Not so; if anyone kills Cain, he will suffer vengeance seven times over.' Then the Lord put a mark on Cain so that no one who found him would kill him. So Cain went out from the Lord's presence and lived in the land of Nod, East of Eden.

The criminal case of Cain and Abel is not yet over. It did not take place in legendary primaeval time; it still keeps going on. Cain keeps killing Abel. Cain must continually be brought to trial. However, one thing has changed since the story of Cain and Abel was whispered to explain the human tendency to become degenerate: Cain's prospects have improved. It is worth going over his trial again. The charge is well known and need not be repeated. But we need to summon new expert witnesses to cast scientific light on his action. We can allow the defence to plead mitigating circumstances. And as the jury, we can decide in our consciences whether or not Cain's condemnation is to be upheld. Here we shall have to listen very carefully to the voice of the judge as we hear it in the biblical text. God speaks four times to Cain. He addresses him directly four times. We have to school our conscience by this voice.

As expert witnesses I suggest a historian, a sociologist, a biologist and a philosopher. Each is allowed two minutes to speak – the philosopher rather more (he finds it difficult to express himself briefly and clearly). But I would ask you to withold the verdict of your conscience until you have heard the experts and considered the judge's four remarks.

Let's listen to the historian first. He declares:

Scholars disagree over the case of Cain. There is a widespread view that Cain is the victim of a bad obituary. The story was told to explain why the 'Kenites' – the descendants of Cain who lived as a nomadic tribe in the south of Palestine and like the Israelites worshipped the God Yahweh – led a restless itinerant life. It was passed on from one set of neighbours to another to explain why the Kenites were different. People in those days did not say 'Neighbours are different', but 'They are bad. They left the cultivated land under a curse because of a crime. That is why they have not settled. But since they too believe in Yahweh, they may not be killed. They are under Yahweh's protection, despite the criminal action of their first ancestor.'

The other view is that while the story may originally have been an expression of lack of love between neighbours, it was included among the sagas of primaeval times. As a result it became a saga about all human beings – just like the story of Adam and Eve. So what once was attributed to neighbours out of prejudice came to be regarded as a possibility for oneself! In the view of the biblical narrator anyone could be Cain. Everyone repeats the story of Cain and Abel.

Thus our historian. And now I ask in Cain's defence whether both explanations do not end up in an acquittal of Cain. If the malice of neighbours towards the Kenites was involved when Cain was accused, must he not be rehabilitated? And if everyone is Cain, can one still condemn Cain without condemning oneself? Judge for yourself in your own conscience!
Now to the second expert. The sociologist says:

Cain is a farmer, Abel a shepherd. They stand for the first division of work at the time of the neolithic revolution, when human beings changed from being collectors and hunters to farming and rearing cattle. They represent any social differentiation up to the present day. With them there is an increase in the unequal distribution of opportunities which escapes moral assessment. Our story expresses this in the account of the sacrifices of the farmer and the shepherd. One sacrifice is arbitrarily accepted; the other is arbitrarily rejected. From this, people in antiquity inferred that things would go well with the former party and badly with the latter. One could count on God's blessing (i.e. on fertility and riches), but the other did not receive a blessing. By contrast, with the help of sociological theories we would now explain the same situation like this: unequal opportunities involve structural violence which kills even when not a single murder takes place. The fact that life expectation in the countries of the European Community is seventy years while in the developing countries it is only forty means that because of different conditions, death strikes there more frequently and earlier than it does among us. The imbalance in social development is a violence which kills. In one and the same human family, related groups are caught up in conditions which make some die earlier than others. And when the latent violence in relationships becomes manifest and the disadvantaged groups rebel against it, their superiors have the more deadly weapons for dealing with this problem.

That's the sociologist's view. And again as counsel for the defence

I appeal to your conscience. Aren't those mitigating circumstances for Cain? What becomes clear from his murder is latent in the unjust distribution of opportunities. Who will cast the first stone here?

But there's a third expert to listen to, the biologist. He asserts:

Cain and Abel have to be put in a wider context. Their story is the story of humankind generally. *Homo sapiens* could establish itself only by outstripping other variants of human life, allowing them to die out or exterminating them. It is far more probable that we are all sons and daughters of murderers than of victims. We are descendants of Cain rather than Abel. For victims have less chance to have offspring than murderers. However, this conflict within our species is harmless compared with the inexorable struggle between the species. *Homo sapiens* has spread over the planet to a far greater degree than any other living being – at the expense of all other living beings with whom we share the same genetic code. We have developed at the expense of other forms of life. Every year many species of animals and plants are irrevocably exterminated. To put it poetically, the earth might say: 'That's it. I've drunk too much blood. Let the blood of the victims be on the head of the perpetrators.' These human beings have destroyed an equilibrium which came into being over millions of years; now they run the risk of themselves becoming the victims of their wanton interventions in nature.

And again I ask you: 'Who can condemn Cain? Aren't we getting close to Cain, so close that we must ask ourselves whether we do not have to identify ourselves with him, even if we repudiate his action? Is the perpetrator better than the deed?'

Our last expert is the philosopher. He argues a daring thesis:

Cain is the first modern man. He rebels against the arbitrary distribution of opportunities: why should Abel be preferred to him? Why should one person be fortunate and another unfortunate? Why should one be rich and another poor? One healthy and another sick? Cain rebels against the view that this is God's will and has to be accepted. His rebellion takes two forms, one destructive and one constructive.

The murder of his brother is destructive. It is reprehensible.

But it has to be conceded that we can understand the intention behind the murder: the metaphysical rebellion against the inequality of human destiny. This most deeply human intention explains why Cain was also capable of more constructive forms of rebellion.

Cain was a builder of cities, and his descendants were smiths and musicians. They brought technical and cultural innovation. They created the material presuppositions for reducing inequality. For only through an increase in our productivity can we do away with the unjust distribution of opportunities in life. Cain is the bringer of progress.

The continuation of the story of Cain and Abel shows that Cain is a rebel, whose destructiveness passes over into constructive action. His aggression is transformed into motivation to achieve, and his criminal energy into a concern for construction. Cain is the first modern man. He rebels because he no longer accepts a religious legitimation for the unjust distribution of fate. He takes the distribution of opportunities into his own hands.

And again, as Cain's defender, I ask: 'Isn't that true? Doesn't this change from destructiveness to constructiveness happen again and again?' I think of the history of Germany. During this century criminal energies of an unprecedented kind were unleashed here, born of simmering experiences of injury and stimulated by a sense of setback. The blood of our murdered brothers and sisters still cries out to heaven. But a little later on the same people go and build cities, achieve miracles in business and culture – yet for all that cannot square their consciences. We are these people. Can we condemn Cain?

Today we have resumed the trial of Cain. We have heard the experts. The defence has made its pleas. Now we, the jury, must consider our verdict. But are we fit to be the jury? Mustn't we be rejected because of prejudice? How can we judge Cain, when Cain's problem is our problem? For the problem of the arbitrary unfairness of opportunities in life is our problem. It is all the more obvious, the more successfully we compensate for inequalities. Let me mention two examples. First, the more accessible our educational institutions are to all, the more painful differences in competence and achievement are felt to be. Every Sunday there are people among us who are consumed by the question: why do the others manage everything so easily and not me? Why do some people find an examination so easy while for me it is an insuperable hurdle? And secondly, the more successfully medicine delays our death, the more bitter it becomes that life-spans are so different. At almost every service there are people among us, including young people, who are preparing for a premature death and fighting with the question 'Why did it happen to me? Why me?'

Cain's problem is our problem, and we must be careful that his destructive answer does not also become our answer. Certainly, it is improbable that we shall kill anyone. But we can turn our destructive aggression against others in different ways. Or against ourselves – in self-destructive depression. We cannot judge Cain. We are prejudiced. It is better for us to hear how someone else judges Cain.

God speaks to Cain four times. Four times we hear his verdict. In this dialogue the saga describes the origin and formation of the conscience. Granted, the conscience is not the voice of God, but it comes into being in dialogue with God. Without this dialogue it remains deaf and dumb.

The first time God speaks to Cain is when Cain is preparing evil in his heart. God says, 'Why are you angry? Why is your face downcast? If you do what is right, will you not be accepted?' This voice does not warn, does not threaten, but makes a promise: 'If you do what is right, will you not be accepted?' That holds regardless of whether we have been given an oppressive or an inspiring lot. It holds regardless of whether we have success or failure with the 'sacrifices' of our work. If we do what is right, we need not feel oppressed, humiliated, hurt, embittered, but we may walk upright. If we follow our consciences, we have an inner compass to guide us even when trees and hills, crevasses and abysses, darkness and cloud veil our sight. The conscience is a guide, but it is certainly not unassailed. For dangers lurk along the way. 'But if you do not do what is right, sin is crouching at your door; it desires to have you, but you must master it.' Yes, you have to master your destructive potentialities. That is a great promise. The whole of human history seems to tell against it. Most opinions and prognoses are pessimistic.

But God intends more for men and women than they suppose. They are to master sin – to master enmity, aggression, envy and destructiveness. We can direct our conscience by this promise – even if it points to a goal which vanishes from our sight in the abysses of life.

The second time God speaks to Cain is after the murder. God asks him, 'Where is your brother Abel?' God asks about the sacrifice, indeed he takes the place of the sacrifice which can no longer speak and asks, 'Cain, what have you done?' Modern men and women are proud of having unmasked the science of the conscience. They are proud of the knowledge that the conscience is not the voice of God but the internalized voice of other people. Our saga sees no contradiction here. In it we hear the voice of God as the voice of the other. But we hear it as the voice of those whom we do not want to hear, those who can no longer raise their voice, as the voice of Abel, the voice of Jesus, the voice of the victims of dictators and oppression. We hear it as the voice of the unborn, against whose interests in life we transgress – as the voice of all the creatures threatened by us. It is true that God's voice is the voice of others, but it is the voice of those who have no opportunity to make a mark on us as a result of our socialization, but who have first to make themselves heard against the internalized voices of others.

God speaks to Cain a third time and delivers a harsh judgment: 'Now you are under a curse and driven from the ground... You will be a restless wanderer on the earth.' Precisely so! Conscience makes one homeless. When the voice of conscience awakens, people become restless wanderers in their lives. They are driven by a restless heart which cannot find rest anywhere. And we can well understand modern experts who say, 'That's too much stress, that causes illness, the Protestant disease, and it is particularly bad when Catholics and atheists catch it.' But let's listen yet again to what God says to Cain. It is an amazing verdict. It is not a death sentence. Simply to say that this is a relic of archaic times, when murderers of members of their family were merely banished and held in contempt, is not enough. For those who told the story of Cain and Abel lived in a society in which murder was punishable by death. Nevertheless they deliberately relate that God punished the first murder only with banishment. Against the legal practice of their surroundings

7

they maintained that God wants the life and not the death of the criminal. Anyone who reads the story of Cain and Abel as schooling for the conscience can learn from it that conscience certainly makes us homeless in this world. We live outside Eden. That is a kind of banishment. But the conscience has no right to kill us. That is not its task.

That becomes even clearer when we listen to God's fourth remark to Cain. Cain complains that the punishment of banishment is too heavy for him to bear. He cannot bear the homelessness, for it means that he is parted from the face of God. 'I will be hidden from your presence; I will be a restless wanderer on the earth,' says Cain. And who would contradict him? The solitary conscience becomes intolerable when it is separated from the gracious face of God, when it is left to itself. Then it can only condemn itself. Then it no longer hears the voice of the one who excuses and forgives. Living with other human beings is intolerable if they can fall upon the guilty. Cain is afraid that as a wanderer he will be killed. Then God says to him, 'Not so; if anyone kills Cain, he will suffer vengeance seven times over.' And God put a protective mark on Cain. Here the idea of vengeance is played off against vengeance. It is not the murderer who will fall victim to blood vengeance, but the one who seeks to exact blood vengeance. We cannot subscribe to this notion, but we can take over the thought that even the murderer stands under the protection of God. God thinks even the guilty worthy of a special sign of belonging. And this sign is to be respected by other people. Cain does not lose his dignity as a human being, since God holds fast to him even after his crime.

We have held the trial of Cain once again. Instead of being the jury we have become the plaintiffs. We have heard the words of the judge – and understood them as a school for the conscience. Can we accept his verdict?

I think that we can accept this:

We are Cain. Cain is not just our neighbour, of whom all kinds of bad things are said.

We are Cain. For as a result of social differentiation we are caught up in a deadly inequality of opportunities.

We are Cain. For we spread ourselves over this earth at the expense of other life.

We are Cain when we rebel against the ethical irrationality of life which arbitrarily favours one and oppresses another.

But God has many plans for Cain, for us. He sets our conscience a great task. He says, 'You must look up. You must walk upright. You must overcome sin. Even if you fail again and again. Even if hatred and envy keep poisoning your life and you find yourselves in the vortex of a destructive tendency towards degeneration. Like Cain you are under God's protection, even when you feel banished from God's sight, when you wander around harrassed and restless in your life. You are all indelibly marked with God's image. You are all branded with the sign of Cain. You are all inviolable. None may make you suffer! None may force you to the ground, for you are destined to look up and walk upright. That is what God has called you to.' Amen.

Jacob and Esau
Or, The un-pious presuppositions of peace

(Genesis 33.1-16)

One of the most remarkable peace treaties in the Bible is the reconciliation between Jacob and Esau. It is not just the end of a family dispute. Both brothers have become one people. Their encounter is a political event. Jacob has sent diplomats to take soundings as to whether he may 'find favour in the eyes of Esau'. They return and report, 'Esau is coming against you with an army.' Jacob expects war. To avert it, he sends a gift in advance, saying to himself, 'I will pacify him with these gifts I am sending on ahead; later, when I see him, perhaps he will receive me.'

Before the encounter with Esau, Jacob has to undergo another contest. A nameless demon falls upon him during the night on the bank of the Jabbok. Jacob is wounded. He limps. But he holds fast to the demon long enough for him to transform himself into the God who blesses. In remembrance of this struggle Jacob calls the place Peniel. This name contains the Hebrew word for 'face'. And he says, 'I saw God face to face, and yet my life was spared.' The question remains open: will he also see Esau face to face, and his life will be spared? That is where the text for this sermon begins.

Jacob looked up and there was Esau, coming with his four hundred men; so he divided the children among Leah, Rachel and the two maidservants. He put the maidservants and their children in front, Leah and her children next, and Rachel and Joseph in the rear. He himself went on ahead and bowed down to the ground seven times as he approached his brother. But Esau ran to meet Jacob and embraced him; he threw his arms around his neck and kissed him. And they wept. Then Esau looked up and saw the women and children. 'Who are these with you?' he asked. Jacob answered, 'They are the children

God has graciously given your servant.' Then the maidservants and their children approached and bowed down. Next, Leah and her children came and bowed down. Last of all came Joseph and Rachel, and they too bowed down. Esau asked, 'What do you mean by all these droves I met?' 'To find favour in your eyes, my lord,' he said. But Esau said, 'I already have plenty, my brother. Keep what you have for yourself.' 'No, please!' said Jacob. 'If I have found favour in your eyes, accept this gift from me. For to see your face is like seeing the face of God, now that you have received me favourably. Please accept the present that was brought to you, for God has been gracious to me and I have all I need.' And because Jacob insisted, Esau accepted it. Then Esau said, 'Let us be on our way; I'll accompany you.' But Jacob said to him, 'My lord knows that the children are tender and that I must care for the ewes and cows that are nursing their young. If they are driven hard just one day, all the animals will die. So let my lord go on ahead of his servant, while I move along slowly at the pace of the droves before me and that of the children, until I come to my lord in Seir. Esau said, 'Then let me leave some of my men with you.' 'But why do that?' Jacob asked. 'Just let me find favour in the eyes of my lord.' So that day Esau started on his way to Seir.

The sagas about Esau and Jacob deal with the conflict between two groups which are at different levels of civilization: Esau is a hunter and Jacob a shepherd, 'a quiet man, staying among the tents'. Jacob represents progress. He has the greater material success. He returns to Palestine with great flocks and herds. But like many representatives of progress he has departed suspiciously far from traditional ethical norms: he has deceived his father, pulled a fast one on his brother and cheated his host. Now he is anxious, anxious that the cheated Esau will have his revenge. Nothing is more likely than that Esau will seize by force what Jacob has deprived him of by fraud.

The biblical sagas take us into another world. But in this world we can sometimes recognize ourselves more easily than in the maze of modern complications. In plain words, we are Jacob. We represent a progressive stage of civilization. The advantage that the shepherd has over the hunter is the advantage that privileged nations have over others. Like Jacob, we are blessed. But like Jacob we have acquired our riches at the expense of others. In order to become rich we have thrown old-fashioned criteria of family solidarity overboard. We have become rich and – like Jacob – homeless. Now we are anxious: will those of whom we once took advantage have their revenge? Will they seize our riches? Our anxiety has a solid foundation: unfair distribution of possessions and the bitter awareness in others that they have been cheated.

Nor am I thinking just of distant developing countries. We meet the problem of unreconciled brothers much closer to home. When I was a student we made a discovery which explains some things that we have done – for better or worse. It was the discovery of being privileged: privileged in having time to reflect, but also privileged that our study was a ticket to the material goods of this world which others did not have. Suddenly it dawned on us that we could not take this for granted. Why did the others let that happen to them? We worked out complicated social theories to explain this. The gist of them was that from early childhood the privileged class pulls a fast one on the others so skilfully that they don't even notice. We were all Jacob who deceived Esau. Some Jacobs became Jacobins. They wanted to ally themselves with their cheated brothers and sisters - an alliance which took increasingly desperate forms, the less they wanted to have to do with us. But most people began shamefully to deny their privileges. The great complaint arose that we ourselves had negative privileges, had been cheated and taken for a ride in university and society. We can understand some things better if we hear behind all that students, all that we have done in the last fifteen years, the bad conscience of the better-off: the bad conscience of the sons and daughters from a good home who discover that all advantages always have to be had at the expense of the losers in our society – who long for a society without losers, for reconciliation with their brothers and sisters. Today we have to note that there has been no reconciliation. In our society the official world and the world of the others, the world of students and intellectuals, is as unreconciled as ever. And that is oppressive.

How can brothers be reconciled? How can there be reconciliation between shepherds and hunters, between the industrial nations and the developing countries, between intellectuals and others?

Let's read the story of Jacob and Esau once again. There is an impressive image in it which keeps recurring: reconciliation is seeing face to face. We can also understand that today. If you can look someone in the eye, face to face, the atmosphere is good. This theme occurs three times, and it illuminates three aspects of reconciliation.

First of all the image occurs in a very matter-of-fact context. Jacob says to himself, 'I will pacify him with these gifts I am sending on ahead; later, when I see him, perhaps he will receive me.' Here there is a material basis to reconciliation: readiness for giving. Then the story makes it clear that giving in itself is not enough. It is just a nice move which reconciles Esau with Jacob before he can press his gift on him. Even then Esau holds him off: 'I already have plenty, my brother. Keep what you have for yourself.' Reconciliation between brothers is easier if both have plenty, if each recognizes the other's wealth: Jacob Esau's wealth from hunting and Esau Jacob's wealth from his flocks. But as I have said, giving away this wealth is not enough in itself. The important thing is how one gives it. What kind of giving is it that creates peace? In our story it is a giving that already presupposes reconciliation, that does not take place just out of anxiety or out of a bad conscience. For in the end Jacob explains his gift like this: 'Please accept the present that was brought to you, for God has been gracious to me and I have all I need.' This giving is a handing on of the common goods of creation which are only lent to each person, which belong to no one. Such a giving can help us to look one another in the face – without being ashamed of the gift, angry at having it pressed on one, without guilt feelings and resentment and without anxiety about rekindling covetousness. But beyond question it is a giving away. For what use are all attempts to look one another in the face if one is not ready to compensate for material inequality? That is the first condition of reconciliation: the first, but not the only one.

The motive of looking someone in the face occurs again in the Jacob story. The nocturnal struggle with the demon has been inserted into the middle of the encounter between Jacob and Esau. It must have something to do with reconciliation. For Jacob says after the struggle, 'I saw God face to face, and yet my life was spared.' To Esau he says, 'For to see your face is like seeing the face of God, now that you have received me favourably' - in other words, my life has been spared. The narrator who brought the two passages together saw a connection here. Let me put it quite generally. Reconciliation between brothers (and sisters) presupposes that we have coped with a nocturnal, grisly aspect of religion, the nightmare of a hostile power which bars our way over the river to where our brothers or sisters are to be found. It is not that we deny or conquer this power, but that we turn it into a blessing, and in the end can be sure that we were not dealing with a hostile demon but with the God who blesses. What happened in the history of the tradition of this saga, the integration of an archaic stratum of religion into belief in Yahweh, in God, is something that we have to keep doing time and again. But what is that archaic stratum, that nocturnal side of religion?

We should not just think back to the Inquisition and the Wars of Religion. They are long past. But absolutist religious mania is still around. Intelligence and education are as little protection against it as ostentatious religionlessness. Those who in 1914 stirred up a war psychosis through a public declaration were prominent German professors of theology. And the people who make political conflicts almost insoluble because religious faith hardens the fronts – in northern Ireland, in Iran, in the Near East – are also intelligent people. The dark side of the tendency towards absolutism is also evident in the message of a Heidelberg citizen who a few steps from here preaches on a house wall, 'Terror makes a good trip!' That is religious enthusiasm which seeks liberation from one's own dead end in the mystical experience of violence. And it's folly. But such folly is not to be found only in some obscure subcultures. The view that either the Eastern states have to conform to our social system or there will ultimately be war sounded more civil put that way, but it is no less disturbing in its hostility to life and far more dangerous when advocated by influential circles. Wherever people argue with absolutist mania for their aims, their social and private forms of life, life is endangered. Reconciliation becomes difficult, almost impossible.

Before Jacob is reconciled with Enoch, he has to overcome the nocturnal demon, must confront him face to face without running away, must hold him fast and acquire his strength. And that is something that we all have to do, particularly those of us who are religious: overcome the absolutist mania in ourselves, the false idols, in order to recognize the God who blesses. Afterwards we shall limp. It is not so easy to forget that the tendency to degeneration to which history and the history of religion bear such abundant witness lies within us. There is no point in making a sharp distinction between light and darkness, between Francis of Assisi and the Inquisition, between the Reformation preaching of the gospel and the wars of religion, between a Christianity which preaches brotherly love and another which allowed the fratricide of the Jews, between one country which produced the *Critique of Pure Reason* and another which built the concentration camps. No, these are the same people, it is the same country, it is the same religion. It is like a curse and a blessing, the nocturnal demon which blocks the way to our brothers and sisters and the God who blesses and opens up the way to them. There will be no peace as long as we deny this nocturnal demon and run after the false idols of absolutist, pious mania.

We must stand fast, compel him till he blesses us. For we have the same promise as Jacob: we cannot set free the powers which the absolutist mania drew to itself, we cannot transform its energy into unconditional motivation for life – and not for death – for a yes to life which is grounded neither in the present form of society nor in a future one, but in the fact that we are creatures and the world is our home, a father's house in which we cannot be lost, in which all life has its rights, even though it may be different from our own.

But reconciliation has yet a third dimension. What is the use of gifts? What is the use of overcoming the pious mania? Reconciliation ultimately depends on the two brothers coming together – and in a very different way.

Jacob approaches Esau with all the ceremonies with which a vassal subjects himself to his overlord: he prostrates himself seven times. Then comes his court, arranged according to protocol: first the serving women, then the women, then the first lady. Tribute is brought. Everything comes to a climax in the address, in which Jacob makes Esau almost a god, as in Eastern court ceremonial: 'To see your face is like seeing the face of God.' Esau's behaviour is in extreme contrast with this. He rushes towards his brother, embraces him and kisses him. He meets him as one meets a brother after a long time. Esau says, 'My brother', Jacob, 'My lord'.

How are we to interpret this contrast? Is Esau the primitive hunter and noble savage, who brushes aside the ceremonial gestures of the cultivated shepherd and produces immediacy? Or is the generous Esau once again falling victim to Jacob's calculating ruses, to his prostrations and his presents?

Let's look at the starting point again. A war is threatening. The situation is tense. Small signals could tip the balance. Petty misunderstandings could lead to a bloodbath. In this situation the signals with which the two sides approach each other have their significance: Jacob's court ceremonial, Esau's family ceremony. Jacob's cautious approach in a way saves the situation: it gives Esau the role of the superior. Esau need not feel threatened. So we should not only praise Esau for proving to be human; we should also praise the impious, deceitful Jacob, whose cautious, step-by-step approach takes the tension out of the situation. We should praise both of them, because they find a way to each other through a great cultural difference, and each accepts the other's ritual.

One could say that these are small details. What role does such a ritual have in great conflicts? On the contrary, in tense situations we need to exchange unambiguous signals of approach, cautiously and step by step. We cannot rush at the other party – either in private or in society or in international affairs. Anyone who preaches 'Throw away the weapons' and starts singing the 'Ode to Joy' misunderstands human possibilities. We must break down mistrust by slow steps – and in so doing expect our signals to be interpreted in very different ways. We must be as cunning and deceitful as Jacob, who takes into account the worst, war, but does not doubt the possibility of peace. And we must be as spontaneous and direct as Esau.

If the two sides have made their approaches cautiously, then reconciliation can take place – not on the basis of the relationship between vassal and overlord, hunter and shepherd, first born and second born, but on the basis of the fact that we are all brothers and sisters. Beyond all the cultural differences there is an elemental bond between human beings. We did not make this bond. It is pre-programmed into creation. In the light of this elemental bond,

Jacob's remark, 'To see your face is like seeing the face of God,' takes on a new meaning. We do not see God's face. We have intimations of God somewhere in the depth of the world. We sense his traces in the mighty cosmos – from the remotest galaxies to the smallest atoms. We sense a central order and experience our own thought and our own creativity as a faint echo of it. We only sense it. But we do not see it face to face. However, when we become reconciled with our brothers and sisters, then for a moment it shines out. Then it is as though we experienced the meaning of the whole universe. Then the encounter with the other becomes a sign of our reconciliation with God. Usually this is only transitory. Jacob and Esau part again. They do not long for total reconciliation, a longing that asks too much of us. It is enough if we can avoid violence and sorrow in conflicts. But it is already as though we saw God's face. For in all these provisional reconciliations what happens to us is what Paul describes with the words:

> Now we see but a poor reflection as in a mirror; then we shall see face to face. Now I know in part; then I shall know fully, even as I am fully known. And now these three remain: faith, hope and love. But the greatest of these is love. Amen.

The Obstinate Prophecy
A Christmas sermon on Isaiah 7.10-16

I often feel that Christmas is like a temporary entry into another world. Everyday life fades. The last gifts have been taken care of. The parents' fight to clear up the home has ended with or without success. Now at last there is peace. It's true that no Christmas is a good one unless it is an entry into another world. But no Christmas is authentic unless it is the incursion of another world into our everyday life, unless something strange reaches out for us that we did not seek, did not wish for, did not buy, did not make. It is my task to bring this truth closer to you. I shall try to do so by retelling the Christmas story. In so doing I shall speak of Mary and Joseph as people of our own time.

Mary and Joseph were a young couple, unmarried; Mary had not finished her education, Joseph had no money. Mary got pregnant; Joseph was not certain whether it was his child. The only certain thing was that his career plans had collapsed. He said to Mary, 'That child is spoiling everything. Go to the doctor. You haven't finished your studies. Nowadays qualifications are very important. Abortion – wouldn't that be the most reasonable solution?' But Mary retorted, 'Who knows what plans God has for this child? Perhaps it has a great task in the world.' And they argued. Joseph thought, 'There are already too many people in the world. If *we* bring a child into this world it should only be if we can guarantee it good surroundings, an assured future, love and security.' Mary protested, 'I can't guarantee anything – and I couldn't, no matter how rich and powerful I was. I only know that I already love this child now. I want it.' Joseph muttered that this was rather irrational, but he saw that he had no right to demand abortion against a woman's will. 'All right,' he said, 'we want the child.'

Now at this time a census was being carried out. It was to be the basis for useful plans: taxes, schools, factories, streets. Joseph thought that was reasonable. Mary was mistrustful, though she conceded that she found it difficult to give reasons for her mistrust when she heard about the good things that went with the census. She asked Joseph, 'Couldn't we smuggle our child through the census uncounted? This child shouldn't have a number.' Joseph muttered that again she was being rather irrational. In the end they would have nothing to fear. He was for basing decisions on solid figures. And he succeeded in convincing Mary to go with the census. However, they were lucky. The child was born at Christmas, and the day of the count was already past. The child remained uncounted.

When the child was a few days old, the young couple had a visit. Wise men from the East appeared and claimed that they were looking in Western civilization for a life which was free from any idea of usefulness, a life which was already good and valuable in itself, a life which in their own language they would call 'holy', if anyone in the West still understood this word. They were convinced that only such a life could save human beings from bankruptcy. In their search they had heard of a child whose parents were said to be called Joseph and Mary. They had looked for him everywhere. And now at last they had found someone whom all the information fitted. Mary said, 'You could be right. The child is no use to us. We don't even know how we're going to feed it.' Then the wise men brought their gifts and gave them to the child. But Joseph noted with displeasure that their words went to Mary's head. Outwardly he remained courteous. Only when they had gone did he shake his head and sigh, 'Typical Mary. Again it's all a bit irrational.'

Now a few days later Mary read in the paper that some politicians had sworn to exterminate irrational thought from society, so that world government could run more smoothly. The swamp in which obstinate ideas grew was to be drained. That made Mary anxious. She said to Joseph, 'We must emigrate. There is no place for me and my child in such a world. I no longer feel safe here.' But Joseph reassured her: 'Our politicians are bound by the constitution. They have sworn an oath to it. We're safe from interference.' But Mary disagreed. She said, 'I once heard an old story. A new king was born, and the ruling king did not know who this new king was. Only that he was born. So he simply had all the children of a certain age killed.' Joseph raised his hands in despair and said, 'Dear Mary, our historical-critical scholars showed these stories up as legends long ago. Nothing like that ever happened, still less can it happen again today. We've developed effective and rational control of power.' But Mary didn't believe him. 'When politicians see that they have to give way to others, when they see their power threatened, then they do the most impossible things – even if they've sworn the opposite under oath and given their word of honour.' And Joseph lapsed into a confused silence: this time he couldn't contradict her.

So perhaps for that reason he gave way. They both studied the maps together to find a country to emigrate to. In studying the conditions for emigration they noted that the richer the country, the more difficult it was to get into, if you no longer felt safe in your own country. Everywhere the laws for those seeking asylum and for refugees had been tightened up, just in the last year. Mary panicked and thought, 'A world with so little humanity is going to fall apart.' And Joseph sighed with resignation, 'If only you hadn't sung those rebellious songs about the God who puts down the mighty from their thrones and raises up the lowly, who fills the hungry and sends the rich away empty! You shouldn't have told everyone that you hoped that your son would do all this. Now they're singing that in the churches everywhere in your name, as the song of Mary. What country will accept people with such subversive ideas? Where did you get them from?' And Mary said, 'From the Bible. There are lots of ideas like that in it. But they're not a danger to the state, only to the politicians who want to put themselves in God's place. And they're a promise for our son, since I hope that it will show him that God is not on the side of these politicians, but on the side of those who are oppressed by them.'

Joseph thought all this utopian and irrational. And they argued over the meaning of the sayings in the Bible. After some toing and froing they decided to look for a biblical scholar who was an expert in the Bible. He would explain everything to them. They were lucky. The biblical expert whom they consulted knew his Bible. He turned up Isaiah 7.10-16, by chance the text I am to preach on today, and made some brief comments about how the text was to be understood.

He explained that at that time a war was threatening in Israel, that Syria and northern Israel wanted to compel the kingdom of Judah under its king Ahaz to enter into a military coalition against

the Assyrians. That they wanted to depose the vacillating Ahaz
and replace him with someone else. That the prophet Isaiah had
prophesied to king Ahaz the collapse of the two hostile kingdoms.
And that Isaiah had offered the king a sign to support his trust in
the prophecy. So Isaiah said to the king:

*'Ask the Lord your God for a sign, whether in the deepest depths or
in the highest heights.' But Ahaz said, 'I will not ask; I will not put the
Lord to the test.' Then Isaiah said, 'Hear now, you house of David!
Is it not enough to try the patience of men? Will you try the patience
of God also? Therefore the Lord himself will give you a sign: The
young woman will be with child and will give birth to a son, and will
call him Immanuel. He will eat curds and honey when he knows
enough to reject the wrong and choose the right. But before the boy
knows enough to reject the wrong and choose the right, the land of the
two kings you dread will be laid waste.'*

Now for a brief version of the explanation the biblical scholar gave.
As such experts tend to do, before he got to the heart of the
matter he first mentioned ten possible interpretations given by his
colleagues. It would take too much time to go through all of them
here, so I shall sum up the main points in my own words.

At that time king Ahaz was afraid that the country would
collapse. Nowadays, too, many people fear that life will collapse: the
economy, strategies for security, the ecosystem, the psychological
balance of human beings. Like Ahaz we are rightly mistrustful of
the promise of great signs and wonders which apparently indicate a
turn for the better. But against our will, against our mistrust, God
forces a sign on us, a sign which takes place time and again and
which we often overlook. The sign is simple and undramatic. A
young woman will bear a child. It will grow up and live – despite all
the threats. And many threats will disappear by the time it is grown
up. As long as we can say 'A young woman will bear a child and it
will grow up,' there is hope. Some people will not concede this. But
some people involuntarily betray that they are unconsciously borne
up by this hope.

Let me try to explain this. We live in a very pessimistic adult
culture. There is much resignation, disappointment and cynicism in
it. But even pessimistic adults shrink from infecting their children

with their pessimism. The morality of our children's books is optimistic. And in bringing children up we do all we can to communicate the belief that life can succeed, despite all threats. Moreover, we also attempt to hand this faith on even if our own faith has been eaten away and undermined. It's as though a sovereign voice challenged our attitudes and insights, saying, 'For every child there is the offer of a good life which you may not attack. Every child has an opportunity that you must not put in question.'

But many people will not listen to this voice. Many people fail to hear it. We are often as deaf and unmoving as stones. And so we are directed to hear this voice in the form of a child, of whom the Bible says that this voice took bodily form in him. The word of God became flesh in him. Because this child was born on earth, this earth cannot be written off. Because this child came into our world, we must not forsake this world to find a good life. Because this child belongs to us, we need never give up the hope that peace is possible.

That was recognized by the politician who promised that he would bring a candle to this child and its mother in Altötting in Upper Bavaria and light it – as a token of gratitude if against all expectations a few rockets were dismantled. This politician has already often spoken the truth aptly, sometimes even involuntarily. I don't know whether he actually did light the candle. But we shall be lighting a few candles later – and then we shall remember with gratitude that for the first time a tiny step has been taken towards disarmament, a tiny step towards peace.

And when we go home and light candles there, we should all remember:

Today, on Christmas Eve, we are asked whether we want to accept this child into our midst. Whether it is to be born in us anew. Whether we say that it's too much trouble and disrupts our plans. Away with it! How many people abort it in their hearts before it can grow up there?

Today we are asked whether we will accept this child as a brother in our midst. If we do, we belong to a family which is not counted in any census: to the family of God in which all are equal and free.

If we accept this child, we discover something that risks being submerged in our civilization, something holy, and perhaps we shall get back into conversation with the wise men from the east.

If we accept this child, we shall recognize that God makes the great small and the small great, and we shall measure the great by whether they are ready to become small – and to let themselves be voted out.

If we accept this child as our brother, then we belong to a family to which refugees and those seeking asylum belong with equal rights. And I am sure that our new brothers will often perplex us with statements like, 'Whatever you did for one of the least of these brothers of mine, you did for me' (Matt.25.40).

Today on Christmas Eve this child presses itself on our family. And he asks whether we will give him a place in our lives. We need not give him anything. He brings his own gift that we cannot buy, cannot organize, cannot make, but can only receive. He makes us certain that God is love and that this love embraces us in life and death – despite everything that prompts resignation, disappointment and cynicism.

If we accept this child, then we do not forsake this world. Another world, a new world, enters into our life and fills us with joy and gratitude. And may the peace of God which passes all understanding, keep our hearts and minds in Jesus Christ. Amen.

Letters to Exiles
Variations on the Letter of Jeremiah

(Jeremiah 29.1,4-14)

This is the text of the letter that the prophet Jeremiah sent from Jerusalem to the surviving elders among the exiles and to the priests, the prophets and all the other people Nebuchadnezzar had carried into exile from Jerusalem to Babylon: This is what the Lord Almighty, the God of Israel, says to all those I carried into exile from Jerusalem to Babylon: 'Build houses and settle down; plant gardens and eat what they produce. Marry and have sons and daughters; find wives for your sons and give your daughters in marriage, so that they too may have sons and daughters. Increase in number there; do not decrease. Also, seek the peace and prosperity of the city to which I have carried you into exile. Pray to the Lord for it, because if it prospers, you too will prosper.' Yes, this is what the Lord Almighty, the God of Israel, says: 'Do not let the prophets and diviners among you deceive you. Do not listen to the dreams you encourage them to have. They are prophesying lies to you in my name. I have not sent them,' declares the Lord. This is what the Lord says: 'When seventy years are completed for Babylon, I will come to you and fulfil my gracious promise to bring you back to this place. For I know the plans I have for you,' declares the Lord, 'plans to prosper you and not to harm you, plans to give you hope and a future. Then you will call upon me and come and pray to me, and I will listen to you. You will seek me and find me when you seek me with all your heart. I will be found by you,' declares the Lord, 'and will bring you back from captivity. I will gather you from all the nations and places where I have banished you,' declares the Lord.

Sometimes I toy with the idea that there is an 'Academy of Sciences' in heaven. In it have been gathered together the wisest of all the wise – from all peoples and nations – and they have been given a task. They are to survey all the texts of world history and select what can be included in an eternal canon of truth. If one could make suggestions for inclusion in this canon, among other pieces I would propose the letter of Jeremiah to the exiles in Babylon. Seldom has faith, love and hope been expressed so convincingly in a biblical text as here. Here are three arguments to support my case.

My first argument is that in this text faith in God becomes faith in the universality of God. In it a revolution in the history of religion takes place. For Jeremiah's contemporaries the God of the land could be worshipped only in the land of Israel, only in the temple of Jerusalem and only with sacrifices. Foreign countries were unclean. The food was unclean, the people were unclean, everything was unclean and caused separation from God. But Jeremiah says, 'You can find your God even in this distant land. You can call on your God even without temple and sacrifice, and he will answer. It is vital for you to ask for God with all your heart – then he will allow himself to be found in a foreign land, in exile, in an unclean land. For God is present everywhere.'

My second argument is that in this letter of Jeremiah love becomes love of enemy. It is addressed to people who have been conquered, humiliated and deported by military force. They are embittered, long for vengeance and dream of an imminent return. To them Jeremiah writes, 'Seek the good of the land to which God has banished you. Seek the wellbeing of the land of your enemies. For their wellbeing is also your wellbeing. Their peace is also your peace. Pray for their land.' It is the very land from which an army is to set forth soon after the arrival of this letter to capture Jerusalem again and to destroy the temple. Here we have an anticipatory illustration of Jesus' command, 'Love your enemies and pray for those who persecute you.' It is also an illustration of the political significance of love of one's enemies. It applies not only to private enemies but also to collective, national enemies. It requires us to think of their wellbeing, their peace, their *shalom*, and to be concerned for it.

The third argument that I would want to present to the wise would be: this letter of Jeremiah is a testament of hope. Israel's exile has become one of the great images of human hope – an illustration of how blessing can emerge from catastrophes and a future from pain. It is no easy hope. Jeremiah warns against prophets of salvation who promise an imminent return. He says that it will take seventy years – in other words, none of those to whom he writes will live to see it. So they are to accept their situation in exile, but not regard it as unchangeable. It will change. Even if over-hasty hopes for change will continually be frustrated, the promise holds: 'I know the plans I have for you,' declares the Lord, 'plans to prosper you and not to harm you, plans to give you hope and a future.'

I hope that these arguments will lead to my suggestion being taken up – if not by an imaginary academy in heaven, at least by you. I hope that you will include the letter of Jeremiah in that private canon in which each person collects the texts that he or she particularly loves or values.

But I would expect even more of my imaginary academy in heaven. Not only that they would publish the selected texts in scholarly editions, with historical and philological notes, but that they would produce valid new versions, revised editions, changed texts, understandable without a commentary. That would be scandalous for an earthly academy: altering texts because one believes that one has grasped their spirit. But other criteria apply up there, so we can entertain the plan of editing the letter of Jeremiah, which was written to the exiles in Babylon between 597 and 587 BC, in three new versions. The first version is to be addressed to all men and women at the end of the twentieth century, the second to the Christian community around 1990, and the third to each one of us in church today. Here are my suggestions for these new versions. Whether they will be given the blessing of the heavenly academy I do not know. For me it would be enough for the academy to think them good.

The title of the first version of the letter of Jeremiah is: Letter of the prophet Jeremiah to men and women at the end of the twentieth century.

Dear fellow human beings of about eighty generations after me, I am writing to you basically what I wrote to the Babylonian exiles. For you, too, experience your world as exile. Your nature is damaged. You have a hole in the ozone layer, your forests are dying, your fields are being corroded by poisonous sludge. You are in mortal danger – since you are set on collective suicide in an attempt to guarantee security against your enemies. You live in an unpleasant world, in a modern world. So you want to put it behind you as quickly as possible – with a trick. Some of you are persuading yourselves that you already live in a postmodern world, that the exodus from modernity has already begun, that the return from exile is already in process.

Do not think ill of an ancient Israelite prophet if he warns against postmodern prophets who promise you a speedy return to what you have lost, who promise you that you can again have as intimate a relationship with nature as in imaginary earlier times which never were. Be warned against the givers of oracles, astrologers who want to activate planetary powers for you in the sign of Aquarius. Certainly you will have to address your contemporaries rather more gently than I did. But I say to you openly, all this is an abomination to me.

Let me tell you, rather, that you have to put up with this unpleasant world. That you should build houses in it. That you should make yourselves useful in it. But you should never forget one thing. This world can change, will change, perhaps not in your lifetimes, perhaps only later. But it is not as final, as irreversible, as it seems.

My concrete advice to you is the same as that to the exiles in my letter. First of all, have children and bring them up. For every child is a confession of the hope that this earth will remain habitable. And every child is a declaration of war on those who make it uninhabitable.

Furthermore, work for peace in this inhospitable world. Your salvation and the salvation of the world are indissolubly bound up together. Its peace is your opportunity of life – for yourselves and for your children. And learn from me that one cannot make peace against one's enemies, but only with them.

Finally, hold fast to hope. Much will change. This world has gone through crises and catastrophes and will continue to do so. But there is hope for it. There are continually opportunities for leading a successful life in it.

So I ask you, do not go into inner exile. Do not fail to show this world the solidarity that it needs, so that life remains livable in it. Fight for its wellbeing. So says Jeremiah, the prophet.

That would be my suggestion for the first new version of the letter of Jeremiah. Of course I have an idea of the complaints heaven will make. They will complain that there is not enough theology in it. But so far I have been speaking only of the world. So here is a second version.

The title is: Letter of the prophet Jeremiah to the Christians of the 1990s.

Dear Christians,

As a Jewish prophet I am reluctant to become involved in Christian concerns. But that is what you wanted. You asked what kind of a message I have for you. I have the same message for you as for the exiles in Babylon. Many of you have experienced the way into the modern world as a way into exile, as banishment from a world in which Christian faith was a natural home for all. Now you live in a world in which you represent a minority – in surroundings which are indifferent to you or reject you. That is a loss which no one should dispute. It is a loss that today even church schools must consider whether to stop school prayers because they meet with only lack of interest or mockery. It is a loss when knowledge of the Bible declines. That must grieve many older people, just as my fellow countrymen were grieved when temple worship ceased after the destruction of the temple. For many people it was as though God himself had been lost. But believe me, God can be found even in your modern world, perhaps far from traditional sanctuaries, remote from familiar religious traditions.

But, you may object, hasn't God been far more thoroughly lost to the modern world than to some Israelites at that time who lamented the loss of temple worship? Is not the universe nowadays analysed without God? And life lived without God? Yes, world and life have been disenchanted. Where once the warm light of God's goodwill shone through the world, it has become cold. The wonders of creation have become meaningless clouds of molecules. But here my question to you is: is it that God is absent or that you are incapable of deciphering the signs which point to him? Is the problem that you only want to have anything to do with signs from which God can necessarily be inferred – and in so doing overlook the signs which point to him? These signs contain an imperative: seek me with your whole heart and I shall be found. They are signs which we only decipher rightly if we are prepared to transform ourselves and allow ourselves to be transformed. Do you not have in your modern world far more signs of this kind than we did 2500 years ago?

Don't you know far better than we did that we are products of a system of nature, the guiding factors in which we shall never completely understand? Don't you know more clearly than we did how the forms of life are constantly reorganizing themselves to match a mysterious reality to which everything must adapt itself, from slipper animalculae to the human brain! Don't you experience much more intensively the lostness of human beings in a giant universe, so that it is all the more miraculous to experience that every human life between cradle and grave has an infinite value, a value which would never emerge from the context of this world? Don't you see much more clearly the boundaries of the world in which you live – that every world is a construct of your senses and your understanding?

Believe me, there are many signs in your modern world. They are like flowers breaking through the asphalt, like the cries of children who disrupt the home, like summer days in October and snowflakes in May. 'If you follow these signs and call on me,' the Lord declares, 'then I will answer you! If you ask after me with all your heart, I will be found by you.'

The problem remains: there are only a few who seek him. And they sometimes don't find it easy when intelligent contemporaries diagnose that they have fallen victim to a kind of religious bacillus which is resistant to the Enlightenment, which cripples them on their way to the modern world. If I, Jeremiah, may say something about that as a Jewish prophet: you Christians have looked down for centuries on us Jews – as being crippled on the way to final salvation, for not wanting to join with you in what you regarded as progress: faith in Jesus Christ. But now your own enlightened children are overtaking you and looking down on you because you do not join in all their 'progress'. Perhaps you now have more understanding of the loyalty with which the Jews held on to their old traditions, against the trend of the time and in a minority situation, compared with which your own situation is very comfortable. Perhaps you will follow their example. That is the message of the prophet Jeremiah to you.

Or more precisely, that would be my draft for a second version of the letter of Jeremiah. I suppose that the scholars in heaven would criticize it for being too abstract in some places: too much advanced theological semantics. That makes my third version of the letter of Jeremiah all the more important, as a personal letter to each one of you.

The title is: Letter of Jeremiah to an unknown worshipper at this church on 23 October 1988.

Dear worshipper,

I don't know you, but I presume that you too have experienced an exile – the loss of your childhood. However fraught it may have been, in retrospect it usually appears as a time when the world was a home. It certainly wasn't the last loss. Perhaps you have experienced separation and divorce from someone you loved. Or you have said good-bye to a phase of life in which you took health for granted – and now you know that it will never be like that again. Or the loss of ideals and goals, or even the loss of faith – how something in you shattered into pieces which can never be put together again as they were. Losses hurt. If they get too much for us, we sink into waves of depression and feel lost. I've experienced that myself, moments in which I was banished from my own life – into an exile more terrible than any exile abroad, a state in which one longs for oneself, longs to return to one's own life, to be at home in it again, instead of standing alongside it like a stranger. It was hell. When it was very bad, I spoke – and you can read it in my book: 'Cursed be the day I was born! May the day my mother bore me not be blessed! Cursed be the man who brought my father the news, who made him very glad, saying, "A child is born to you – a son." Why did I ever come out of the womb to see trouble and sorrow and to end my days in shame?' (Jer.20.14-18).

If only at that time I had had a wife to comfort me! But precisely that was denied me. God forbade me to marry. He forbade me to take part in friendly celebrations. I was to be a gloomy prophet of judgment. Day after day I was isolated, and at night I lay alone in bed. I became a depressive!

And yet I survived. That's why I'm writing to you. I want to try to make clear to you what helped me to survive. It was the love of God. That sounds very romantic, but it is something very unromantic. I felt his love in the fact that I had a task which only I, the prophet Jeremiah, could fulfil, a task for which God needed me. For that is his love, that he gives us a task, that he makes demands on us. I had to prepare my people for its catastrophe – and after the catastrophe strengthen its hope. That is what I was chosen for from my mother's womb.

I'm certain that you too have a task between cradle and grave, a task which no one can fulfil but you, a task which only you can decipher – no one else in your place, not even me.

You say, 'But I am so small, so helpless, I can't do anything.' That's not true. Only you can accept your life as God's gift. No one else. Only you can see the opportunities in it. No one else. Here you're not helpless, nor are you too small. You're the only one who is competent.

Perhaps you'll say, 'But I'm often only a poor old thing, happy to survive the winter.' I tell you, even if you're terminally ill and the shadow of suffering darkens your life, you can have a task – to bear this fate. And perhaps you have an opportunity here to bear witness to something that transcends this suffering. Just read my lamentations and confessions. Read Job's complaints. Read the account of Jesus' passion. They all say that a message can be contained in suffering to which you alone can give the answer.

Never forget that God has entered into a covenant of life with you. How can you say that you're worthless? If he makes you an instrument of his peace for just one individual, how can you say that your life is useless? Even if you were born into a great darkness and light only a tiny candle in it – how can you say that you were dispensable, superfluous? You're a thought of God. You'll never fully decipher this thought, but you may be sure that it's a thought of salvation and not of damnation. For God's promise, 'I have loved you with an everlasting love; I have drawn you with loving-kindness', applies to you too. You can read this promise of God in the book that my disciples put together, in chapter 31. They rightly collected the essentials of my message to you. So says the prophet Jeremiah.

Will the heavenly academy adopt this letter? You needn't worry your heads over that. If his message has reached your heart, it was a good letter. And if it has not yet penetrated your heart, then wait. One day the message will come. It is addressed to you, to you personally. So I dare to say to you, to all of you, 'May the peace of God which passes all our understanding keep your hearts and minds in Jesus Christ.' Amen.

Jesus as Exorcist
A painful story?

___

(Matthew 12.22-30)

Then they brought him a demon-possessed man who was blind and mute, and Jesus healed him, so that he could both talk and see. All the people were astonished and said, 'Could this be the Son of David?' But when the Pharisees heard this, they said, 'It is only by Beelzebub, the prince of demons, that this fellow drives out demons.' Jesus knew their thoughts and said to them, 'Every kingdom divided against itself will be ruined, and every city or household divided against itself will not stand. If Satan drives out Satan, he is divided against himself. How then can his kingdom stand? And if I drive out demons by Beelzebub, by whom do your people drive them out? So then, they will be your judges. But if I drive out demons by the Spirit of God, the kingdom of God has come upon you. Or again, how can anyone enter a strong man's house and carry off his possessions unless he first ties up the strong man? Then he can rob his house. He who is not with me is against me, and he who does not gather with me scatters.'

Who still believes in demons? Among us, a few backwoodsmen; in other societies, almost everyone. That was also the case in Palestine. Jesus believed in demons. He cast out demons, as Voodoo priests still do in Haiti and charismatic healers in Africa. Furthermore, Jesus attached great value to these exorcisms. He said, 'If I cast out demons by the finger of God, the kingdom of God has come upon you.' There is no doubt that Jesus belongs with painful clarity to the guild of exorcists. But what we do in the case of comparable phenomena today is also painful: we don't drive the demons out of people, but drive people out of our society – into psychiatric hospitals, where we cope with their misery through tranquillizers and medical files. We have demythologized demon possession so

33

that it becomes sickness – and do not even get suspicious when some psychiatrists assure us that this concept of sickness, too, is only a myth by which modern societies label deviant behaviour, helpless about really understanding it. So we shouldn't be arrogant about cultures which believe in demons and drive them out.

Nevertheless, within the framework of our cultural convictions we must be clear what we understand by 'demons'. Only then can we understand why casting them out can be a realization of the kingdom of God. Hence our first question: what are demons?

I should tell you from the start that I don't believe in demons. Or, to be more precise, I believe that demons have their still largely unexplored abode somewhere between neurophysiological structures, social conflicts and psychological pressures – not only among some 'sick' people, but among all of us. The readiness to see demons and react to them is there in all of us. Imagine that you're walking all by yourself at night through a dark wood. You're a modern person. You're psychologically stable. Nevertheless you'll feel a propensity to see ghosts and demons. There's a rustling in the bushes. A gust of wind changes the trees into infernal organs. A shadow falls over you from the right. We're again in the jungle, with the constant threat of wild animals who see better in the dark than we do. Demons and ghosts are projections of wild animals who hunt by night, of which our ancestors of millions of years ago were so afraid. So there are relics of an atavistic readiness in all of us to see life-threatening demons where they do not exist.

Granted, we usually have such levels in us under control. But sometimes the world turns into a hostile jungle even for us. Probably everyone has experienced this at some time in a dream. Friendly faces turn into persecutors. We can't escape. Our enemies are quicker.

Or we experience it waking up – when a nightmare is upon us. Colleague XY seems like a ferocious monster, against whom one has to defend one's territory. Bureaucrats become packs of wolves, snuffling after opinions. Young people turn into anarchists, hitting out at everything. It all gets tremendously distorted. Reality is distorted by hostile projections. Predatory beasts prowl through the soul. Then morning comes. The sun shines. The ghost disappears.

Colleague XY greets us warmly. Young people are young people. Bureaucrats are bureaucrats. A table is a table. We're back in the everyday world.

But can't we imagine how some people never get back to our everyday world? How they remain in the world of the atavistic jungle, where everything has a hostile significance? We talk learnedly of paranoid symptoms – but perhaps we should simply say that they, the others, could no longer make their way back from a world in which we are all immersed for a while. Can we take it amiss if our poor fellow human beings remain there? Aren't they perhaps experiencing the world from a realistic perspective? Can't whole societies lapse into that atavistic state in which human beings become wolves, in which all the filth that we can normally control mounts high? We've experienced it in Germany: at that time the marauding beasts didn't just prowl through the soul. Nightmares came true. Since then we have come to know that demons – as projections of an atavistic readiness to react – are alive in all of us. They threaten us all. We are all threatened by the danger that projections which see other power blocks as primal predatory beasts may disengage our political reason. We are all threatened by the danger that projections conditioned by the jungle will paralyse social reasoning in our own countries. And above all there is the danger that an unhappy combination of both processes will lead to the collapse of our civilization.

If demons are projections of anxiety conditioned by the jungle, we can answer the second question thrown up by our text: why does the expulsion of demons represent the coming of the kingdom of God? Why can Jesus say, 'If I drive out demons by the Spirit of God, the kingdom of God has come upon you'?

This saying belongs in a particular historical situation. At that time it was the Romans whom people wanted to drive out. They were the hated occupying forces. The supporters of the resistance movement hoped that God would then rule alone. Then 'God's monarchy' would begin. That is reminiscent of Jesus: he, too, preached the kingly rule of God. He even hoped that it would begin to come about through his activity, regardless of whether the Romans were still in the land or not. That is why the way to the rule of God was so different in each case. The resistance fighters were convinced that one had to launch planned attacks on the Romans to bring about the 'sole rule of God'. Jesus, however, was convinced that 'If I drive out demons by the Spirit of God, the kingly rule of God has come upon you.'

Jesus is not fighting against the Romans, but against demons. Jesus does not kill anyone to further the coming of God's kingly rule. He heals people.

Jesus provisionally accepts Roman rule, but not the rule of atavistic projections over people, projections in which Roman rule was also expressed. A demon in the New Testament does not speak Latin by chance. He proudly calls himself Legion. If we lived in a society which believed in demons, they would speak Russian or American. For demons usually come from the other side of the border.

In short, Jesus does not want to create order on earth by force, but order in the brain. I think that is relevant today. Peace largely depends on whether we succeed in creating order in our brains – or whether we give way to that atavistic readiness to react in us which sees the 'others' as the enemies who threaten life, who threaten us in the jungle of the world.

But here the question 'How?' is decisive. Jesus' opponents raise a necessary question: does Jesus drive out demons through Beelzebub, the lesser devils by the chief devil? And that brings us to a third question which in our language runs like this. Does Jesus simply replace the domination of old projections with new more dangerous ones, the old anxiety by new anxieties?

Indeed there is a great danger here. Jesus' opponents were right. Anyone who wants to drive out the atavistic hostile projections must be sure not to put even more devastating hostile images in their place. Anyone who realizes that anti-Communism is an attitude which is hostile to life should not replace it with anti-Americanism. Anyone who sees how our hostile images are bound up with our social order should be totally against this order. The existing institutions of the politics of equilibrium are an imperfect way of keeping the peace. But those who reject these existing institutions and see them as the great enemy or the Antichrist should consider whether they are not driving out the demons through Beelzebub. They make me, at any rate, anxious that they are encouraging the very chaos that they want to avoid. I should add that I also get anxious when I see how politicians in East and West jeopardize what have become institutions of the politics of equilibrium through foolish speeches and actions. We must be sure that we do not replace the old projections of anxieties with new ones, that we do not drive out Satan through Beelzebub.

How does Jesus respond to this charge of being allied with the devil? He recalls the simple insight that a kingdom divided against itself cannot stand. If we drive out the old demonic projections with new ones, our form of life will not be able to survive. What happens to all forms of life which develop organs and patterns of behaviour incompatible with reality will happen to us: we shall die out. We shall not be able to stand. But at the same time Jesus makes a positive statement. He says: I am not driving out the demons with new demonic forces but with the Spirit of God. That is another power. With it comes God's kingdom. The positive side of the exorcisms is the nearness of God, which Jesus expressed in two images: God is the king whose rule is already dawning. God is the father who makes his sun shine on good and bad alike. We should understand such images not as dogmas, but as invitations to see the world in a new light. From both pictures we learn something of that Spirit of God which vanquishes the demons.

The image of the kingly rule of God shows us that the world is not a jungle but is on the way towards becoming an ordered kingdom. Our reason is not alone in the cosmos. It is the echo of a far superior reason, of which our thought and action is only a weak and imperfect reflection, and it gradually discloses itself to us. Indeed, it is still in the making. Let us take Jesus at his word: where the demons are vanquished, the kingdom of God begins. We should take that as literally as possible. Where a psychiatrist conquers paranoid anxieties, there is the kingdom of God. Where men and women overcome their hostility to others, there it is. Where societies develop institutions which make it possible for us to be independent of atavistic reactions, it is beginning. We overcome in ourselves that atavistic readiness to react which conjures up enemies and demons everywhere – and the kingdom of God begins, just as the fruit is already contained in the seed.

And now to the image of the father. The world is not a hostile jungle: it is like a parental home in which we may feel secure despite all the terrors. No one is lost. I know that the image of the father is often criticized as infantile, as though feelings of security and relaxation focussed on our parents and rooted in our childhood were here transferred to the whole cosmos. But what tremendous progress this image represents, compared with those images of the jungle which keep breaking through in the religions! In my view there is only one possible way of not casting out the demons by Beelzebub, i.e. by new projections of anxieties and hostile images, namely being borne up in our fight against atavistic projections by a basic trust that overcomes this anxiety. When that happens the world will again appear to us as a parental home – perhaps it may be a difficult home, but it will be home.

So I don't think that it is a good thing for us Christians to come together and sing in unison, 'I'm afraid, you're afraid, we're afraid.' Anxiety is an important alarm signal, and contributes to survival. But it can quickly become a phobia which threatens life, a compulsion which people of old attributed to evil demons. Our task is, rather, on the one hand to accept anxiety as an important alarm signal – and if necessary even to reveal it and provoke it, but on the other side to counter anxiety with a basic trust. For we have the promise that we will be able to deal with our projections of anxiety. We can conquer them. We are not alone. We have an ally.

Such basic trust is not an assurance that everything will go well. Trust in God is no guarantee against the collapse of our civilization. What we accept for the lives of individuals, without getting into a panic, will one day be true for our civilization:

All men are like grass,
and all their glory is like the flowers of the field.
The grass withers and the flowers fall,
but the word of our God stands for ever.

Everything comes to an end some time. Perhaps when after millions of years the sun becomes a red giant. No one quite knows. But we have to prevent the possibility that our world will perish because of our own inability to vanquish demonic projections of enemies, that it will be destroyed because we have been guilty of neglect over enlightenment, because the demons in us lay it waste and make it uninhabitable. The struggle is therefore worth while. It is also worthwhile because of its aim. For a feature of the mystery of faith is that it can note this end in tranquillity – and yet know that we are absolutely safe, even without knowing why and how. For faith, the world is no longer a jungle with wild animals lurking everywhere. The 'wild animals' in it have been driven out by Jesus. With him the creation becomes bright again. It becomes home. Within it we experience a peace which passes all understanding. May this peace of God preserve your hearts and minds in Jesus Christ. Amen.

Dealing with Religious Prejudices
The example of the Canaanite woman

——

(Matthew 15.21-28)

Leaving that place, Jesus withdrew to the region of Tyre and Sidon. A Canaanite woman from that vicinity came to him, crying out, 'Lord, son of David, have mercy on me! My daughter is suffering terribly from demon-possession.' Jesus did not answer a word. So his disciples came to him and urged him, 'Send her away, for she keeps crying out after us.' He answered, 'I was sent only to the lost sheep of Israel.' The woman came and knelt before him. 'Lord, help me!' she said. He replied, 'It is not right to take the children's bread and toss it to their dogs.' 'Yes, Lord,' she said, 'but even the dogs eat the crumbs that fall from their masters' table.' Then Jesus answered, 'Woman, you have great faith! Your request is granted.' And her daughter was healed from that very hour.

The story of the Canaanite woman is one of the finest miracle stories in the Gospels, but difficult to preach on. It addresses themes which often turn out badly in conversations.

It's about a woman. Nowadays whenever men – especially as theologians – say anything about women and religion there is often a suspicious atmosphere, as though some people are waiting for them to reveal their chauvinism.

The story is about a pagan woman. Jesus is a Jew. Conversations about our relationship with Judaism are still burdened with mistrust – above all mistrust of ourselves. We are now discovering many pernicious traditions in Christian statements about Jews. Who can guarantee that people will not also note their influence in our own words?

The story involves the relationship between rich and poor peoples. Mark calls the Canaanite woman a 'Greek' of Syro-Phoenician origin – in other words, she belongs to that tiny Hellenized upper class in the east of the Roman Empire which we also find in the cities of Tyre and Sidon. For her, Jesus is one of those backward backwoodsmen who were exploited economically by the richer cities. Two worlds meet here, rich and poor – or, as we would put it, the First World and the Third World.

The story also involves three social relationships burdened with prejudices: between male and female, Jew and non-Jew, rich and poor countries. Conversations about these often get bogged down in an unhappy atmosphere because they are burdened with unexpressed prejudices which I could caricature like this:

1. Show me that you have no prejudices and I will take you seriously.
2. Where your view differs from mine, it is because of your prejudices.
3. What you say is right, but you say it too emphatically. You keep having to hold down prejudices in yourself.
4. Even if you're right in what you say and feel, you're in no position to say it: you're a male, a well-to-do white. So shut up!

There are perfect programmes for being unhappy with one another. I've just sketched out one of them. It's very popular in theology and the church (and elsewhere). We shouldn't broadcast it today, but choose another programme contained in our history, a programme for dealing with prejudices.

In this story it is Jesus himself who adopts a prejudiced attitude. A desperate woman comes to him, a foreigner. She asks on behalf of her sick daughter, but is turned down, first by the disciples, which is tolerable, and then by Jesus, too. And that's not all. She is humiliated. Jesus says that he is not available to foreigners. It isn't good to take away the children's bread and throw it to the dogs. 'Dogs,' says Jesus. You have to be pious in an almost unexceptionable way not to find that shocking. To call a person a 'dog' (in whatever form) has always been an insult. Here all exegetical attempts at improvement are a waste of time and show that even the moral sensitivity of some Christian exegesis has 'gone to the dogs'.

Why doesn't Jesus behave like other Jewish miracle workers?

Like Elijah, who helped the widow of Sarepta? Like Elisha, when he healed the Syrian Naaman? Why this rejection of a foreigner? What would we say of a German doctor who refused to treat a Turkish child – and sent away those who asked for his help with hurtful words?

We shouldn't try to convince ourselves that the story didn't happen like this, that it was made up by an early Christian community in which opposition to the Gentile mission was expressed and overcome. That's certainly how the story was once understood. But did it come into being for this purpose? I doubt it. Wouldn't it have been wiser for the community to have attributed resistance to the Gentile mission to the disciples – and to have made Jesus give it the go-ahead? Be this as it may, the first Christians attributed a prejudiced attitude to Jesus. We can't get round that.

Perhaps the story helps us to gain a less prejudiced relationship to our prejudices precisely because of this. If even Jesus had prejudices, who could claim to be free from them? If even Jesus depends on someone else to rid him of prejudices, who wouldn't also be ready to help themselves get rid of prejudices? That's the point of this story. Barriers are erected – but they are overcome. There are inhuman words, but human actions.

So we ask: how can this story become our story? How can we change it in such a way as to recognize ourselves in it? Let me make three variations in the story, so that we can creep into it.

Here's the first variation. Imagine someone with three W-factors, who is white, Western and well-to-do. However, he's not a revolting person. On the contrary, he's aware that his own culture needs cleaning up. He doesn't know what guidance in life to give his children except the bleak slogan, 'Life is short, so let's attempt to make money even quicker.' He doesn't need to compromise himself personally by broadcasting this slogan. There are some politicians who see to that well enough. Our man thinks that what people used to call the 'soul' is now a dark hole, a void, a gap. Once people were concerned that the Spirit of Christ should dwell in it, but now it's occupied by new spirits, and not just good spirits.

So he stirs himself and goes to other continents to discover the Spirit of Christ. He discovers this in a people which is in process of bringing about a non-violent revolution. He discovers it in Christians who live with the lost children of Latin America. He discovers it in the black people of South Africa, who wait in vain for the conversion of their white brothers and sisters, yet devote all their efforts to avoiding the catastrophe which threatens. The life of these Christians is full of humiliations and deprivations. They have no bread, no freedom, no security – but they don't lack the Spirit of Christ.

So our man goes to a wise man among them and asks, 'Give us something of this spirit to make us and our children healthy.'

But he is turned away. 'We've already given you enough. You've plundered our material riches, destroyed our social order, branded our culture as inferior. And now you come and ask us to clean up your washed-out Christianity. Leave us in peace. We're grateful enough to keep the fulminations of your theologians and Congregations of Faith at bay.'

Does this variant fit our biblical story? Yes it does. The Galileans of the backward country region had to provide bread for the rich cities, even if they themselves had too little. We can sympathize with a Galilean when he says, 'It's improper to take away the bread from one's own children and give it to strangers.' We can understand him when he says, 'It's not good for one of these rich foreigners to come and ask for help, as though they weren't notorious for plundering the land and making it helpless.' You can't just ignore a history of bitterness.

And now to a second variant of our story. Our man has understood that centuries of exploitation cannot simply be ignored. No one releases us from our history. So he looks in his own history for traces of the true God, who is not entangled in his history of domination and oppression. He looks in Europe for a city where there are still Jews, and there he visits a wise rabbi. He says: 'I'm looking for the true God among you Jews. For centuries as a persecuted and oppressed people you have borne witness to God: you have borne witness that the true God is not a God of the ruler and the oppressor. Now I have just discovered that this God is also my God.'

But here too our man gets a cool reaction. 'For centuries you didn't want to have anything to do with us. You've already taken so much from us without asking: our Bible, our promises, our ancient history. Now you want to invade our history since the end of the second temple, too. But it isn't your history. You haven't had our suffering. On the contrary, you were the cause of it.'

Our man replies, 'But we're still your children. Christianity is a daughter religion of Judaism. Can't a mother forgive her children?'

The wise man laughs and says, 'What mother wouldn't do that!' But then he becomes serious again and adds, 'But suppose the mother has just survived an attack on her life which – to put it carefully – the daughter could have prevented.'

Our man returns again. He has understood that God has a special history with the poor, the weak and the oppressed. But it is not his history. Rather, his history cuts him off from this history.

The third variation has to be told in the subjunctive. It's only a possible story. Imagine that our man had a wife. Perhaps this wife acts like the Canaanite woman in our story. Perhaps she has more success. She isn't one (or isn't just one) of the winners. She's also one of the losers. Above all she has more experience in patiently overcoming barriers, sometimes with subversive patience. So perhaps she stirs herself. But this story can't be taken any further, because it can't be taken from the pulpit into the streets. We shall have to be patient a while longer until a woman is standing up here in my place. Perhaps she will be able to give the story an ending. So I shall go back once again to the biblical story, which has been handed down in the indicative. How did the Canaanite woman manage to overcome barriers manned with prejudices – even in the case of Jesus?

First of all, it is important that she recognizes these barriers. She doesn't deny them. Yes, she says, that's how things are between Phoenician Tyrians and Galilean Jews. There's a great divide. You might compare it with the divide between human beings and beasts, between children and dogs – but even so, from this perspective there's still a connection: in eating there is a symbiosis between children and dogs. Scraps fall from the children's table for the dogs.

This woman also hears a promise in what Jesus says, despite all appearances. She hears that children are infinitely valuable, far more valuable than dogs. Why shouldn't that also be true of her child? Why shouldn't her child be able to activate the high esteem for children contained in Jesus' dismissive and cynical remark? She hears a promise in the brush-off. Through the prejudice she detects the verdict which binds the other and which she can affirm.

Jesus sums up her conduct in a single comment, 'You have great faith,' he says. Faith here simply means an unswerving trust that another can exercise healing and helping power through personal application. This faith is great because it overcomes deep-rooted antipathies in the other person.

With her faith which overcomes frontiers, this woman has rightly become the model of faith. For this faith overcomes barriers both between human beings and between human beings and God. Or to be more precise, it overcomes those barriers which are the worst of all barriers between people, those barricades people build up by referring to God. Here is a series of variations on the theme 'I am sent, but not to them!'

Christians have all too often behaved in pernicious ways on the basis of this slogan. They have all too often said:

We are sent – but not to those groups which are fighting for their human rights.

We are sent – but not to the workers who must struggle hard for their place in this society.

We have a task – but not on behalf of persecuted Jews.

All too often it is still said that the church is sent to preach the gospel – but this isn't good news for those who suffer under a racist dictatorship. That's only a political question!

It is inhuman to say, 'We are sent – but not to them', and here we're like the Canaanite woman. First we can go on telling ourselves that it was only the disciples of Jesus who ignored the cry for help and turned away the one who sought it. But then the suspicion grows in us that there could be a deeper basis for this human failing. It could have its foundation in the centre of faith. It could occur in Jesus himself, in God himself. God himself encounters us as one who rejects, as inhuman, as an enemy.

We're then in the right mood to be able to understand Paul. Confronted with the view that since Christ God's ways excluded the Jews, he said: I would rather be cursed and separated from Christ than assent to such an inhuman statement. We may also say the same thing. I may also say the same thing on behalf of many people:

45

I would prefer not to be a Christian rather than to give assent to inhumanity with a theological foundation.

But let's keep to the Canaanite woman. Her faith is so great that it breaks through even the barriers of such inhumanity. Jesus recognizes her faith – a faith which puts him in the wrong. What kind of a faith is that? Where does it get its power from? The answer is much simpler than some people may think. It is the faith of a woman fighting for her suffering child. It is an unconditional protest against all the suffering that motivates this faith. This faith is a faith that moves mountains, a faith that overcomes prejudices, a faith that measures everything by an unconditional obligation, the obligation to diminish suffering. This faith gives us the right to contradict the highest theological authorities, even Jesus himself, the Bible, God. Wherever we know that theological convictions and Christian traditions result in suffering, we have the right and duty to contradict them.

Perhaps you will say, 'Can we still believe in such a Jesus, a Jesus who is not perfect, a Jesus who is put to shame by a foreign woman towards whom he has behaved inhumanly?' I think that this is the only Jesus whom one can trust. We can only trust a Jesus who allows a woman to draw him out of his prejudices. Only in such a Jesus do we recognize a human face. This is a Jesus who allows himself to be baptized by another Jew to obtain the forgiveness of sins. It is the Jesus who will not let himself be addressed as 'good master', because only one is good, God – no one else. He is the Jesus who accepts that a woman is right and allows himself to be put to shame. He is the Jesus who told the parable of the two sons.

'A man had two sons. He went to the first and said, My son, go and work in the vineyard. "Yes," he replied, but did not go. Then he turned to the second son and said the same thing to him. He replied, "I'm not going." Later he changed his mind and went. Which of the two did his father's will?'

Jesus did his Father's will in the case of the Canaanite woman. And if we too repent and act as he did, we also have his promise that we shall become children of our Father in heaven, who makes his sun rise on good and bad alike and makes the rain fall on the just and the unjust. May this God give our hearts a peace that passes all understanding and keep our hearts and minds in Jesus Christ. Amen.

The Sign Language of Baptism
Or, Human destiny: The freedom to be children
of God

———

(Matthew 28.18-20)

*Then Jesus came to them and said, 'All authority in heaven and on
earth has been given to me. Therefore go and make disciples of all
nations, baptizing them in the name of the Father and of the Son and
of the Holy Spirit, and teaching them to obey everything I have
commanded you. And surely I am with you always, to the very end of
the age.'*

We baptize this child in the name of the Father, and of the Son and
of the Holy Spirit. Let me try and say in my own words what that
means.

We baptize in the name of the Father. That means that we are
born into this world without anyone asking whether we want to be
or not. One day this child, too, will recognize, 'I have been born
into this one family – alongside millions of other families. I have
been born into this one country – alongside many other countries.
I have been born on this tiny planet – alongside billions of planets
in the immeasurable universe.' Most of what we find there was not
made by us. We can't change our bodies, we can't change the laws
of nature. We can't turn back time. We can't detach ourselves from
our persons. In many respects we are free. But in all this we remain
radically dependent. We may be oppressed by these thoughts, but
we can also sense a meaning in them, as though this were not a
hostile world into which we have been smuggled, but a world which
we can affirm. As though we had a task which we have not formulated
ourselves. As though behind everything that happens, from the
remotest systems of the Milky Way to the tiniest particle, there were

47

a reason, of which our reason is only a faint reflection. If we feel so secure in creation, then we can baptize this child in the name of God the Father, who is the mystery of this world.

At the same time we baptize this child in the name of the Son. What does that mean? It is now secure in its mother's arms. Both parents give it a trust in life on which it will draw to the end. But its trust will be shaken. Two problems will oppress it, with which no one has come to terms: innocent suffering, i.e. injustice, hunger and compulsion, and suffering in ourselves, of which we ourselves are the cause. For we all have an image of what we should be and would like to be, but we know that we do not correspond to this image. No one can spare a child this pain later: shock at the meaninglessness in the world and disillusionment about oneself. But on this earth it has a friend, Jesus. In fellowship with him it can arrive at the certainty that something is stronger than the meaninglessness in and around us: the love of God which has become visible in Jesus as love of humankind. This love removes sorrow where it needs to be removed; this love reconciles us with ourselves, although we live at odds with ourselves. So we baptize this child not only in the name of the Father, but also in the name of the Son, in the name of Jesus.

Finally, we baptize this child in the name of the Holy Spirit. This child now has many people to love it. But it will experience that on this earth one is often alone. It will be afraid of death, which everyone must face alone. It will be anxious about the future. But it should know that a power goes out from Jesus which assures us that we are never alone, that we are safe in a community in which no one is lost – not even through death – a community which has hope for the whole world, even when the future is dark. The church seeks to make this community visible: through shared learning, shared celebration and shared helping. So we baptize this child in the name of the Holy Spirit, the Spirit of hope and community, which overcomes human isolation.

We have expressed the fact that this child is a child of God through an action involving water and words. We have baptized it. What consequences does that have?

One thing is immediately clear. If human beings are children of God, they are not just children of their parents, of those who bring them up, of their country. No human being can lay complete claim to them. They belong to God. The New Testament expresses the freedom given here by speaking of 'sons of God' (in the case of everyone, girls and boys, women and men). Originally in Israel only kings called themselves sons of God. That had consequences. If only the king as son of God had a direct link with God, everyone was dependent on him – so 'son of God' was a title by which kings claimed power and privileges. In the communities which lived with the Bible something revolutionary now happened: not only the king but little people were to be 'sons of God'. All Christians claimed as it were to be kings. And in so doing they claimed indirectly that no other person, no king nor ruler, ultimately had power over them. A Christian is free and independent.

'Children of God' have a second characteristic in addition to freedom. They are loved. I John says: 'How great is the love the Father has lavished on us, that we should be called children of God! And that is what we are!' (3.1). This is God's love, unconditional love. But what does that mean? It is not difficult to love small children as long as they are small and charming. But they grow up. No one knows what they will turn into. Perhaps they will become great. Perhaps they will prove difficult people. Perhaps they will bring their parents much joy. But perhaps they will become a burden – through sickness and handicap. Unconditional love means that they are loved in any case, regardless of how they develop. That's not easy, even when development is 'normal'. As parents we often pin unconscious hopes on our children. Often we expect them to achieve what we failed to achieve: to attain a status that we failed to attain; to realize a marriage which in our case failed; to rebel where we did not have the strength to. Probably we love our children in the hope that they will live up to our unconscious expectations. That is human love. It is not the unconditional love visible in Jesus, which affirms everyone, regardless of whether they live up to our expectations or not. If we allow ourselves to be seized by this unconditional love we may be confident that our problems will be solved – and will not unconsiously expect them to be solved by our children. Then we become free for one another – when parents and children recognize and understand one another as 'children of God'. So to be a child of God means to have freedom over against all earthly authorities – and security in this unconditional love of God. We assure children through baptism that they are such children of God.

But why do we give this assurance through a symbolic bath in water? In former times, at baptism people were completely immersed, so Paul could interpret baptism as a dying and living with Jesus, as a twofold sign of death and life.

Let me explain both. When our oldest child was just two years old, we had to part from him for the first time, to prepare for a move. We took him to my parents. There were a few tears as we said goodbye, otherwise all went well. But the next night I had a dream. I dreamed that the child was in a pool of water and in danger of drowning. I wanted to help but couldn't – and had fearful guilt feelings. I woke up in terror. When I talked about this dream next morning with my wife, it became clear to me what it expressed. I had guilt feelings because we had left our child for the first time. Consciously it had not been difficult for me to leave him with my parents. But unconsciously things looked quite different. In this dream the water was a sign of death, the threat of danger, a sign of parting. When we baptize a child in church, we indicate that this separation is unavoidable, indeed we affirm it because it is the beginning of new life. Just as the child is physically separated from its mother at birth and becomes independent, so in life it will gradually part from its parents. At every parting it is as though something died in us. We are anxious about losing the child. Something in us wants to keep our children for ever. But if we accept the images of immersion in water and new life deep down in us, we become certain that these gradual separations are a transition to a new life. They are not loss, but gain. We needn't be anxious about them. For as a child of God this child is destined to freedom and independence.

That brings us to the other side of the double sign of baptism. Water means not only separation and death, but life, just as in the course of evolution life began in the water. We are fond of associating the renewal of life with the purifying power of water. As surely as water takes away all taint of the past, so despite all failure in the past we may continually begin all over again. We need this promise particularly as parents. When you have children you are overwhelmed with good advice on all sides, and not just from friends and relations. You read books about bringing up children. You hear people talking about bringing up children on television, often very wise people. And as you listen to it all, you get anxious. Can I be a good parent? Then you hear that children need love and friendship. But do you have the nerves for that? Children need balanced parents. But aren't you often moody? Children need stimulating parents. But who is always stimulating? The more clearly one recognizes what children really need, the plainer it becomes how difficult it is to become a good father, a good mother or a good educator. In time you become more modest in your aims. Indeed, there are parents who secretly think themselves failures, who once began with lots of idealism but soon found that they couldn't be ideal parents. Sometimes people don't acknowledge that. Then they seek culprits: situations, or society as a whole, or their partners. Or they secretly blame the children for being so difficult.

It's very important for us to see that we can never be ideal parents. We all do something wrong. But baptism says – as the New Testament says elsewhere – 'Don't despair, either consciously or sub-consciously. You may have self-confidence, even if you make mistakes – sometimes serious mistakes. You may acknowledge them to yourself without having to accuse others. You may always begin again. For there is something that is stronger than all failure and guilt: the love of God, that unconditional love which has become visible in Jesus. Baptism wants to assure us of this love – which seeks to give us independence from other people and confidence in ourselves, although we get so much wrong. Baptism contains this message for everyone, both children and grown-ups. It assures everyone that they are children of God. It says to all of us, 'You are free from other human beings, but safe in the love of God.' Amen.

Help as a Representation of God
And the renunciation of fantasies of omnipotence

(Mark 9.14-29)

When they came to the other disciples, they saw a large crowd around them and the teachers of the law arguing with them. As soon as all the people saw Jesus, they were overwhelmed with wonder and ran to greet him. 'What are you arguing with them about?' he asked. A man in the crowd answered, 'Teacher, I brought you my son, who is possessed by a spirit that has robbed him of speech. Whenever it seizes him it throws him to the ground. He foams at the mouth, gnashes his teeth and becomes rigid. I asked your disciples to drive out the spirit, but they could not.' 'O unbelieving generation,' Jesus replied, 'how long shall I stay with you? How long shall I put up with you? Bring the boy to me.' So they brought him. When the spirit saw Jesus, it immediately threw the boy into a convulsion. He fell to the ground and rolled around, foaming at the mouth. Jesus asked the boy's father, 'How long has he been like this?' 'From childhood,' he answered. 'It has often thrown him into fire or water to kill him. But if you can do anything, take pity on us and help us.' 'If you can?' said Jesus. 'Everything is possible for him who believes.' Immediately the boy's father exclaimed, 'I do believe; help me overcome my unbelief!' When Jesus saw that a crowd was running to the scene he rebuked the evil spirit. 'You deaf and mute spirit,' he said, 'I command you, come out of him and never enter him again.' The spirit shrieked, convulsed him violently and came out. The boy looked so much like a corpse that many said, 'He's dead.' But Jesus took him by the hand and lifted him to his feet, and he stood up. After Jesus had gone indoors his disciples asked him privately, 'Why couldn't we drive it out?' He replied, 'This kind can come out only by prayer.'

'Everything is possible for him who believes.' That is an impossible statement, since only of God can one say that everything is possible for him. Only of God is it proper to say 'He can do everything'. But here a predicate of God is transferred to the believer. Jesus expects people in faith to have a share of God's omnipotence. That sounds absurd.

And yet sometimes we can relate this promise to ourselves. We can do so when we are confronted with the hopeless need of another person, with a need like that of the epileptic boy. He has a spirit which has robbed him of his speech, i.e. he is cut off from human communication. He hurls himself into fire and water, i.e. he behaves in a way which does him extreme damage, self-destructively. Inability to communicate and self-inflicted damage – we also discover this suffering in quite normal people, indeed we find these tendencies in ourselves. In the face of such need the cry sometimes wells up in us, 'If only we had God's power to give new life – in the face of pernicious self-destruction! If only we had God's power to restore desperately divided and embittered people to human society! If only we had a tiny touch of divine omnipotence to prevent the suffering of a single innocent child – or the inexorable decline of a person into death!' Yes, confronted with such need we would like to be omnipotent. Then we would like to hear the promise, 'All things are possible to him who believes.' But precisely at that point we note our limitations, like the father in our story. We feel our unbelief; we feel just how far we are from being omnipotent, how impotent we are to help.

Must we not respect these boundaries? Isn't the wish for omnipotence an irresponsible fantasy? Don't we make grotesquely excessive demands on ourselves if we think that we can take God's place – even just for a moment, to help others?

While reflecting on this I was reminded of the hasidic story of the good side of denying God. It's about human beings taking God's place.

Rabbi Moshe Loeb said: There is no property nor power in human beings which was created in vain. And even all the lower, degenerate properties can be elevated to serve God. Like arrogance: when it is elevated it turns into great pride in God's ways. But what may the denial of God have been created for? It too can be elevated into helpful action. For if someone comes to you and asks you for help, it is not for you to receive him with a pious word, 'Trust, and cast your need on God.' Then you should act as though there were no God, but only one person in the whole world who can help this person, you.

Along the lines of this hasidic story we can perhaps say that as helpers we become God's representatives. At least we should not tell ourselves, 'With God everything is possible. God will help.' What we should say is, 'Everything is possible to those who believe. Help our unbelief.' But how do we arrive at this faith which for a moment makes us God's representatives to others, without succumbing to fantasies of omnipotence?

It is no coincidence that the story speaks of a father. Parents are the first representatives of God. They represent God when they comfort a child in the night who is terrifed and afraid. They take the place of God when they say, 'It's all right. Go back to sleep. All's well.' Taken literally, one can't subscribe to that any more than to the statement, 'Everything is possible to him who believes.' For taken literally, all is not well. Taken literally, much is so disturbing and terrifying that we hardly have any words for it. While we are here together, perhaps in China yet more students are being executed for wanting no more than democratic control of power and despotism. That's terrifying. Nevertheless, we feel it legitimate that at the same time parents somewhere are saying to their children, 'All's well.' That's like an echo of the words which God spoke at creation, 'And behold, all was well.' If other people are to be able to say that also, we must sometimes be God's representatives for a moment. Indeed parents have to be God's representatives to their children – just as the father is to his poor son. But basically it's too much for us. There's no doubt about that.

It's also too much for the father in our story. Jesus does the healing in his place. He takes the place of the one of whom one can say, 'Everything is possible for him who believes.' The formulation here is deliberately ambiguous. The statement can refer either to the father or to Jesus. For the father comes with the request, 'If you can do anything, help us.' And Jesus replies, 'If you can? Everything is possible to him who believes.' The father would like to have this faith. But he detects only unbelief in himself. So Jesus takes his place. He represents God and the father. He represents us where in the face of screaming need we desperately wish, 'If only we had a touch of God's omnipotence so that we could help!' We must learn from Jesus how we can represent God.

I've just asked whether it isn't too much for us to slip into the role of God's representatives as helpers. A first answer is, 'Yes. it would be too much for us, were we not ready to have someone else to represent us. It would be too much if we didn't accept that we are two things. We are the image of God which represents God to all creatures and fellow human beings, endowed with so great a task that it must be a joy to wake up every day and be human. And at the same time we are poor creatures, who find it far too much to cope with the tasks with which we are faced, dependent on someone else's taking our place. And we can learn that from Jesus, who is God's representative to us and our representative to God.'

My second answer also begins from Jesus. We are not only to learn from him how to let him represent us, but also how we are to represent God actively to those who suffer – even if often we cannot help by removing suffering and relieving need. But even then, we can represent God as Jesus has represented him to us, simply by being near to others in suffering. It would be grotesquely beyond us to represent the omnipotent God to others, but not the God who hides himself in suffering and the anguish of death. He is the God whom Jesus represents to us, a God with a human face, who is not omnipotent, but himself cries out, 'My God, my God, why have you forsaken me?'

So if you are confronted with need, remember the story of Rabbi Moshe Loeb. Don't say, 'God will help.' Complain instead that God is so distant. Why does God allow it all, the decay of the body, the decline into addiction and dependence? Why doesn't God put an end to human cruelty? But remember that perhaps God has put you in this place so that you may represent his love to this one person. So that you may represent it just like Jesus, not as a perfect human being, but as one who also suffers and is tried. You are thought worthy to represent God. You are thought worthy to represent the love of God to those who suffer, the only power which does not ask about utility and cost but affirms each person unconditionally and holds them fast as his image, even when other human beings have abandoned them.

Of course you're right if you say, 'I'm not Jesus, I'm not Mother Teresa, I'm not Albert Schweitzer.' Of course you aren't. But think of this hasidic tradition: 'Before his end Rabbi Sussya said, In the world to come people will not ask me, "Why weren't you Moses?" They will ask me, "Why weren't you Sussya?" '

Think of it this way. God has not left it for imaginary people to represent his love to his creatures and help them, but for real people like you and me, people who are themselves dependent on being represented, people who often don't know the next stage. If we firmly believe that God has irrevocably allied himself with people like us to bear witness to his love, then we have a share in a touch of his omnipotence. Amen.

The Proclamation to Mary
An antimyth to the story of the lustful angels

———

(Luke 1.26-38)

In the sixth month, God sent the angel Gabriel to Nazareth, a town in Galilee, to a virgin pledged to be married to a man named Joseph, a descendant of David. The virgin's name was Mary. The angel went to her and said, 'Greetings, you who are highly favoured! The Lord is with you.' Mary was greatly troubled at his words and wondered what kind of greeting this might be. But the angel said to her, 'Do not be afraid, Mary, you have found favour with God. You will be with child and give birth to a son, and you are to give him the name Jesus. He will be great and will be called the Son of the Most High. The Lord God will give him the throne of his father David, and he will reign over the house of Jacob for ever; his kingdom will never end.' 'How will this be,' Mary asked the angel, 'since I am a virgin?' The angel answered, 'The Holy Spirit will come upon you, and the power of the Most High will overshadow you. So the holy one to be born will be called the Son of God. Even Elizabeth your relative is going to have a child in her old age, and she who was said to be barren is in her sixth month. For nothing is impossible with God.' 'I am the Lord's servant,' Mary answered. 'May it be to me as you have said,' Then the angel left her.

Since the early church, Mary has been interpreted as the counterpart of Eve. Through Eve, it was said, sin came into the world, and through Mary the Redeemer. Today, too, I want to read the story of Mary as a counter-story – as a contrast to the myth of the fall of the angels, through whom evil came into the world. First of all let us remind ourself of Mary's story.

An angel comes to Mary from heaven. He announces to her the birth of a child without sexual intercourse. An ancient reader, familiar with stories of heavenly figures who left behind 'sons of

God' on earth, would inevitably have thought: so she has her child by the angel. To avoid this idea it is stressed that Mary will be made pregnant by the Holy Spirit, through a divine miracle, and not through a man or an angel or any form of sexual intercourse. Because of this miraculous origin the child will be called 'son of God'. He will rule as a king over Israel. Mary sees in the fact that she will bear the future ruler as a woman of the people a declaration of war by God on the powerful and violent – a paradoxical declaration of war, since the new king is not to bring war and fighting, but peace on earth.

I don't want to demythologize this fine story here. That often leaves only a pale notion behind. Rather, I want to explain it in the framework of a world which thinks in terms of myths – as an antimyth to the story of the fall of the angels. At that time people used this myth, rather than the story of Adam and Eve, to explain the invasion of evil into this world. There is a brief allusion to it in the Old Testament (Gen.6.1ff.), but it was only developed and worked out imaginatively in the two centuries before the birth of Christ, in the Jewish literature of the time.

In this myth, too, angels descend from heaven. As sons of God they seduce the women on earth and through them beget the giants, the violent and mighty ones of the world, who hurl the world into a cosmic catastrophe. For God sends the flood as punishment for their evil deeds. And had God not saved life in the ark, then all life would long since have disappeared. The story of Mary (and of Elizabeth) can be read as a counter-story to that, at three points.

The first point of comparison relates to the sons of God and the one 'Son of God'. In the myth of the fallen angels, too, angels intervene in earthly events. They, too, beget sons of God who emerge as rulers. But these do not save the world, do not promise peace, but hurl it into a catastrophe. Why? The myth of the fallen angels tells us. The sons born to the human women whom they have seduced are rulers who allow themselves to be worshipped as sons of God and disseminate dangerous weapons on the earth. It does not take much historical imagination to interpret that: the 'invasion' of the angels runs parallel to the invasion of the foreign rule of Greeks and Romans. Greeks and Romans brought previously unknown techniques of war to Palestine. Their rulers had themselves worshipped as gods. Their hybris is attacked in the myth of the fall of the angels. In the form this myth took at the time it is a retort to the advance of Hellenism, a challenge to the blurring of the boundaries between the human and the divine in pagan culture.

The story of Mary reads very differently. She too bears a 'son of God'. But this son of God does not bring any military power on earth. He brings the promise of peace. This son of God is not worshipped as divine because of his political power but goes the way of helplessness to the cross – and yet he is superior to all warlike powers.

The second point of comparison relates to the women who are seduced and the one woman 'Mary'. The myth of the fallen angels is a mischievous denunciation of women. The fallen angels introduce spells and magic into the world – in short, witchcraft. And they are particularly successful with women. Perhaps this reflects the attractiveness of Hellenistic culture to women: this new culture did bring them some improvements – along with a deep undermining of traditional patterns of behaviour and rules and a vehement repudiation of the new by traditional forces. With the repudiation of the new culture, a misogynistic trait entered the biblical traditions which also had an influence on the New Testament. We all know the not very redeemed-sounding arguments with which Paul justifies the covering of women's heads. This is necessary 'because of the angels' (I Cor.11.10). Here Paul means the fallen angels of the myth. Covering the head is meant to ward off and deter these lustful, seductive angels. We trace the demonization of women in such remarks – with ominous consequences down to the present day.

The story of Mary also appears as a counter-story against this background. Here God allies himself with a woman, a son is begotten by divine power, but no demonizing male fantasy distorts the image of Mary (and Elizabeth). Mary and Elizabeth are ordinary women – they have no abnormal powers, no witchcraft, no magic. Nor do they need to be protected against them.

Unfortunately Paul did not know these stories. Otherwise, how could he really have been able to write that women must cover their heads to deter the angels? Would he not have had to say that angels can approach a woman without her being led astray? Yes, an angel can approach her and even announce the begetting and birth of a child. And this can play a role in redemption. Thank God, one might say, Mary didn't wear any covering on her head that might have kept the angel away! The angel came to her. She was alone with him. He did not seduce her. He did not beguile. He simply told her God's word.

If we read Mary's story against the background of the story of the fall of the angels we can get a sense of the tremendous power in it, directed against the demonization of women.

Some people will ask critically, 'But doesn't this amount to a transfiguration of Mary (and thus a positive mythologization of the woman) which we cannot accept either?' For whether someone is stuck in hell or lives in heaven the result is the same: they disappear from human company.

That leads to a last point of comparison. The boundary between heaven and earth is blurred in both stories. In both stories a boundary is crossed which otherwise is insuperable. In the myth of the fallen angels it is crossed by sons of God seducing women on earth – in the story of Mary by an angel announcing a miraculous birth. The word of God breaks through the boundaries between earth and heaven. Of this God it is said at the end of our text, 'Nothing is impossible with God.' And Mary says, 'I am the Lord's servant, may it be to me as you have said.' We are all directed towards this saying in the same way as Mary. And we are all directed to this saying in the same way. Mary, who hears the word of God and trusts it, is neither the demonized woman nor the mythically transfigured woman. She is our sister, because like us she hears the word of God.

The evangelist Luke expresses that in two sayings of Jesus about Mary which speak for themselves.

As Jesus was saying these things, a woman in the crowd called out, 'Blessed is the mother who gave you birth and nursed you.' He replied, 'Blessed rather are those who hear the word of God and keep it' (11.27f.).

This idea was so important to the evangelist that he introduces it a second time. He tells this story at another point:

Now Jesus' mother and brothers came to see him, but they were not able to get near him because of the crowd. Someone told him,

'Your mother and brothers are standing outside, wanting to see you.' He replied, 'My mother and my brothers are those who hear God's word and put it into practice' (8.19-21).

This word of God is a creative power. It produces life. It begets in Mary the Son of God. It breaks through the boundaries between heaven and earth. It promises peace on earth – and the raising up of the poor, the hungry and the lowly. May this word of God also show itself to us as creative power. May it create in us new people so that we all become sons and daughters of God, sisters of Mary, brothers of Jesus. Amen.

The Our Father
A summary of essentials

(Luke 11.1-4)

One day Jesus was praying in a certain place. When he finished, one of his disciples said to him, 'Lord, teach us to pray, just as John taught his disciples.' He said to them, 'When you pray, say:

> *Father,*
> *hallowed be your name,*
> *your kingdom come.*
> *Give us each day our daily bread.*
> *Forgive us our sins,*
> *for we also forgive everyone who sins against us.*
> *And lead us not into temptation.'*

That even the disciples had to learn to pray is a comfort for modern men and women who have difficulties with praying. However, if we look closely, we see that the disciples didn't have our problems. Their request, 'Lord, teach us to pray, just as John taught his disciples', betrays another motive: they want a prayer which distinguishes them from other groups. Luke mentions the baptist groups as a comparison, Matthew the Gentiles. The Our Father is to differ from their 'babbling' by its simplicity and brevity. In another early Christian writing, the Didache, it is the Jews from whom the Christians distinguish themselves with the help of the Our Father.

But the Our Father is the least suited prayer conceivable for distinguishing us from others. Any Jew and any Muslim can recite it, and probably it would not be difficult for many Hindus to say it with us. It is a quite basic prayer which concentrates on the important things between cradle and grave.

And yet it has become the prayer of Christians. And I would like to take seriously the awareness that we encounter in the various early Christian texts: the awareness that this prayer is a special treasure entrusted to Christians – a treasure for which we could give away a good deal as long as we find it. Its special feature is precisely this concentration on essentials. It sets out what we can contribute to the dialogue with all religions: to the dialogue with Jews and Gentiles, believers and atheists. It sets out what we may hope to receive assent to from others – supposing that we have previously introduced this prayer into our own lives, supposing that we find in this prayer the convictions by which we can live and die.

I shall suggest for each clause of this prayer an idea which is particularly important to me. I begin with the form of address, 'Father'. This address is as it were the bracket which holds together all the petitions. When I was a small child, my father was at war and a prisoner of war. I didn't get to know him until I was six and a half years old. Before that I knew him only from stories. God may be like that for some people. God is absent. Many people know God only from stories. And they hope that God will enter their lives later so that they can feel that something in these stories rings true. It rings true that we do not owe our existence to chance, but to a power who wanted us with love, who gave us the task of living, who affirms us and supports us in good days and in bad. Some people may say that with our parents, father and mother, we remain within our sphere of existence. But with that father we go beyond it. What can we already know of him? How can we trust him? Let me recall something very simple here. Even in the case of earthly parents, one thing radically escapes our experience: the story of the love between our mother and our father, that story in which our own existence has its human ground. We can only hear of it. Indeed we even have to take the identity of our father and mother on trust – on the basis of stories of others. But it is reasonable here to believe and trust that it was love – or at least the longing for love – which helped us to exist. If we trust that, then in later life with our parents we shall find much to confirm and justify this faith, and we shall also not allow ourselves to be led astray by the inevitable conflicts with parents, or even by long alienation. But if we are full of mistrust, if we suspect that we owe our existence not to a love story but to something else – calculation or chance or thoughtlessness – then we shall also find much to justify our mistrust. That is how I imagine our dealings with God: we relate to him as we do to our father and mother. If we trust the accounts which tell us that we owe our existence anew each day to a love story, then every day we shall have new experiences in which this trust is confirmed. And it is quite reasonable to have this trust – even through deep crises and catastrophes.

Now let's go through the petitions in detail. 'Hallowed be your name.' God is present everywhere. But he is not recognized everywhere. He often remains anonymous – without a name, without praise and thanksgiving. Here too I would like to make a comparison: our self is always present in our lives. It is quite impossible for us to escape it. But it is not always conscious. We become aware of it only in some situations which tear us away from our usual routine: only then do we become aware of the fact that we are irreplaceably ourselves, this one person between birth and death, who has to make decisions which no one else can make – and encounter joys and sorrows that no one else can have. Similarly, God is always present in our life. But only in a few situations does he emerge from his anonymity, does he disclose himself, so that we ourselves become the answer to his call, with body and nerves, ideas and actions – and at the same time terrified that we owed him this response. Where God emerges from his anonymous, nameless present, we experience one thing above all: that we must change profoundly, that we must 'hallow' ourselves (as one can say in biblical language) in order to correspond to him and to hallow his name, so that he is not driven out, not forgotten, not despised.

That's not all. We go on to pray, 'Your kingdom come.' That means that to correspond to God not only must we change ourselves, but the whole world must become different, so that it emerges from its anonymous present and can be lived in. That was one of the great discoveries in the Bible and in Judaism: the world which corresponds to God, in which his name is acknowledged and hallowed, cannot be the same as the world which now exists, which seems to be so final – and which is nevertheless only a transition in the great process of reality. This new world, which will fully reflect God's presence, is not something incomprehensibly remote. It already begins in hiddenness here and now. It already began in Jesus. And also in

Francis, in Gandhi and in Albert Schweitzer. In all these figures something is present of that kingdom of God in which God's will is done not only in heaven but on earth.

But now we live in a problematical world which is different from that world in which God's will prevails. In this world we must pray, 'Give us each day our daily bread' – or, as we should probably understand the phrase, 'Give us each day tomorrow's bread', so that we are freed from tormenting cares about life. For precisely that is the great temptation to which we are exposed in this world. Bread is scarce. Material goods are limited. We are born into a hard struggle over the distribution of resources, a struggle at the heart of which is deep distrust that there may not be enough for everyone. If we trusted that there was enough for everyone, it would not be so hard for us to give something away. But as it is we fight over the scarce goods of life – between classes, between nations, between generations, between developed and underdeveloped countries. No one escapes this oppressive context: we all live at the expense of other people. Indeed, we now discover to our horror that as a human species we live at the expense of all other kinds of living beings. We have spread over this earth so successfully that countless species are already extinct and many more die out each year. That is what I call the inexorable struggle over distribution. In it we have a right to life, to the bread we need to live. We also have a right to tomorrow's bread. But what we are now doing is more: we are consuming the bread for the day after tomorrow. We are plundering the planet so that those who live after us will not find much left, and we are letting the hungry beside us go away empty.

So it is necessary to pray, 'Forgive us our sins, for we also forgive everyone who sins against us.' We are all guilty in this struggle over the distribution of food and opportunities, for even if we are personally innocent, we are caught up and entangled in a system of unfair distribution. We darkly suspect that there is a close connection between the catastrophes of famine on this earth and our luxury. We also suspect that our ordered (and perhaps indeed successful) life and study are connected with the failed and ruined lives in our society: where there are winners there are also losers. The rules of the game are often unfair. But those who take part in the game confirm them – even involuntarily.

Precisely this insight is a great temptation to cynicism. And so we pray: 'Lead us not into temptation.' The tempter approached Jesus in the wilderness loaded with biblical quotations. It's the same with us: incontrovertible truths become our temptation. It is an incontrovertible truth that life is a struggle over distribution, that we have great difficulty in escaping this struggle, that all civilization limits it only up to a point, that it would be too much for the conscience if we felt personally responsible for all that goes on. And then along comes the tempter and whispers all these truths in our ear – and suggests that cynicism which says, 'If you personally have your share in this struggle over distribution (your share of food, education, possessions and status) – why bother about the fate of others?', and he goes on to whisper, 'It's really time that you rid yourself of your post-pubertal dreams and faced reality.' We are mostly tempted by truths, sometimes even by truths supported by science. But the temptation is that we forget the most basic things.

We forget that we owe life to the power of God. Before God and through God we all have the same right to life.

We forget that we are constantly called to repentance, so that his name is hallowed through our actions and thoughts.

We forget that we are all caught up in that process which is aimed at changing of the world, so that everyone can experience God's goodness.

'And lead us not into temptation.' Today, that means 'Lead us not into temptation to deny the reality of God.' For in that case everything could basically remain as it was. In that case we could persist in our laziness, and the world in its remoteness from God. Amen.

On Changing Human Beings and the World
A Bible study on Mark 13.28-37; Luke 13.6-9

Now learn this lesson from the fig-tree: As soon as its twigs get tender and its leaves come out, you know that summer is near. Even so, when you see these things happening, you know that it is near, right at the door. I tell you the truth, this generation will certainly not pass away until all these things have happened. Heaven and earth will pass away, but my words will never pass away. No one knows about that day or hour, not even the angels in heaven, nor the Son, but only the Father.

Be on guard! Be alert! You do not know when that time will come. It's like a man going away: He leaves his house and puts his servants in charge, each with his assigned task, and tells the one at the door to keep watch. Therefore keep watch because you do not know when the owner of the house will come back – whether in the evening, or at midnight, or when the cock crows, or at dawn. If he comes suddenly, do not let him find you sleeping. What I say to you, I say to everyone: 'Watch.'

Then he told this parable: A man had a fig-tree, planted in his vineyard, and he went to look for fruit on it, but did not find any. So he said to the man who took care of the vineyard, 'For three years now I've been coming to look for fruit on this fig-tree and haven't found any. Cut it down! Why should it use up the soil?' 'Sir,' the man replied, 'leave it alone for one more year, and I'll dig round it and fertilize it. If it bears fruit next year, fine! If not, then cut it down.'

The two parables of the fig tree are images of hope. The parable in Mark says: The world will change. As surely as the fig tree will become green, so God will change the world. The parable in Luke is an assurance that people can change. Even if they look like a withered tree trunk, God gives them a chance. The possibility of changing the world and human beings – that is our theme.

The fig tree is an apt image of this hope for the transformation of the world and of human beings. Unlike most trees in Palestine it loses its leaves in winter. It stands there ike a dead tree, but puts

67

out new leaves so regularly in the spring that the seasons can be distinguished by it. The fig tree is an image of hope – even where everything tells against hope, where everything looks dead.

But I don't want to use this fine image to get round a less fine problem, which has long concerned me. In connection with the parable of the budding fig tree Jesus says, 'I tell you the truth, this generation will certainly not pass away until all these things have happened.' By 'this generation' he means the generation of the time. According to the Gospel of Mark this great change is to be expected soon. At the beginning of the Gospel Jesus appears with the message, 'The time has come. The kingdom of God is near. Repent and believe the good news!' Here it is clearly said that the great change will happen very soon, indeed that it has already begun. But we now know that the kingdom of God did not come. The church came, and that was a disappointment compared with the kingdom of God. For has the world been changed by the church? Have people got better? Have wars stopped? Didn't a criminal history of Christianity also begin with it from which we must turn with sadness and horror?

The New Testament bears witness to a great hope for the transformation of the world and human beings. But it bears witness to a disappointed hope, indeed to a mistake. When that dawned on me during my theological studies, it affected me deeply. It was not a new insight. Already at the end of the last century scholars had seen that a great hope was disappointed in the New Testament. It was immediately clear to me as a student – and I haven't changed my mind since – that how we deal with this insight is a touchstone for our honesty and sincerity in dealing with the Bible. Let me go on to tell you how I have struggled with this question from my student days on. I can distinguish three phases. But I should begin by saying that in reality my development was far more chaotic than the division of this Bible study into three sections suggests.

The first phase came in the 1960s. When I was studying then, the New Testament was being zealously 'demythologized'. That means that many remarks about the world and history were regarded as outdated. The sayings about the end of the world or a miraculous change to the whole world were among them. In essence, it was said, such statements about the wider world referred to the little world of each individual between birth and death. For everyone is his or her own world history. A world history is buried under each tombstone. The decisive issue is whether in this little world history, in you and in me, a great change takes place between cradle and grave, whether there is repentance, a change in attitude. The world needs to be renewed radically in each individual follower of Jesus, in each Christian. In the New Testament this changing of the individual was imagined as a changing of the whole world. But the essential thing is what happens in personal life, in your own existence. And since existence was a fashionable word at the time, the whole approach was called 'existentialist'.

In my 'existentialist' phase I learned to interpret biblical texts with all the methods of the art, and also to compare them with other texts. In looking for parallels to Luke's parable of the fig tree I came across a fable of Ahikar, a wise man from the ancient Near East, who is said to have lived at the Assyrian court. Many sayings were in circulation under his name in New Testament times. They included this fable, which a father tells to his misguided son:

My son, to me you were like a palm tree which stood by the side of the road, but no one plucked fruit from it. Its owner came and wanted to tear it up. Then the palm tree said to him, 'Give me another year and I'll produce saffron for you.' Its owner replied, 'Wretched tree! You didn't produce your own fruit; how can you produce a different fruit?'

This fable of Ahikar begins from a presupposition which is also familiar to us from the Jesus tradition. A tree can only produce certain fruits. A palm tree can only produce coconuts. A thornbush cannot produce grapes, a thistle cannot produce figs (Matt.7.16). Either – we read elsewhere – the tree is good, in which case its fruits are also good, or the tree is bad, in which case its fruits are also bad (Matt.12.33). Here a tree appears as something fixed and unchangeable. It cannot suddenly bring forth quite different fruits – or fruits that are substantially better than before. And as the tree and its fruits are an image of human beings and their actions, that means that in these sayings of the Jesus tradition human beings seem to be fixed. A good person does good. An evil person does evil. Therefore you can know people by their fruits. For there is a fixed connection between tree and fruit, between a person's being and actions. Here we encounter what is basically a very pessimistic view of human beings, a view like that in the fable of Ahikar: essentially, human beings cannot change. The more I was convinced at that time that the biblical message should lead to a change in the individual, the more this pessimism became a source of great doubt for me. Here are three of my problems.

The first problem is that since their appearance in this world men have always killed other men in war. Up to now that was taken for granted. In the heroic epics of all peoples the killing of other men in war is quite naively glorified. How are human beings to be permanently capable of living without wars – although they have to learn this in order to be able to survive? Can one expect a predatory beast to live without catching prey? Can one expect a thistle to bring forth figs? Or human beings to ban war for all times?

The second problem is that human beings have so far always drawn boundaries around themselves. The rejection of foreigners, those of another language, other customs, other convictions, with skin of another colour – this rejection is deeply rooted in us; it is almost a kind of instinct. Now – for the sake of internal and external peace – we must learn to accept foreigners without hesitation and to regard them as part of ourselves. But can we do that? Can we overcome the archaic heritage of xenophobia?

And the third problem is that if we look at the history of the world, human beings have always ruled over other human beings and the rulers have exploited their dependents; political rulers have oppressed others, landowners have exploited others, men have lived at the expense of women. And all that has also been justified and defended with Christian notions. Will we ever learn to get beyond this state of dependence?

For me, that the individual must and may change has hitherto been one of the great truths of the Bible. In my existentialist phase this was the heart of Christianity for me. But it was also the very cause of the problems I have mentioned, which are in fact the same problem. We clearly sense that to overcome them we would have to achieve quite new modes of behaviour, beyond all that hitherto has been regarded as normal. We want that with all our hearts. We long for it. But aren't we like the palm tree in the Ahikar fable, which makes quite flippant promises, as though it could produce a fruit which can only grow on quite a different tree? As though it could produce the aristocratic saffron instead of ordinary coconuts?

The image of the tree and its fruits contains a deep conservatism and pessimism in its very structure. A tree remains a tree. A man remains a man. For that very reason it was an important discovery for me that this image of the tree is used in a new way in the New Testament – in contrast to the traditional image. It begins with John the Baptist. He speaks of the 'fruits of repentance' which everyone is to bring forth. Without such fruits of repentance the axe will be laid to every tree. That's a bold image. Have you ever seen a tree that repented? A tree that was converted? I haven't. On the contrary, trees are the embodiment of something that remains in one place. Nevertheless, John the Baptist uses this image, which unites two irreconcilable things: trees and repentance. Trees cannot repent. Only human beings can repent.

Jesus was a disciple of John the Baptist. He learned the image of the tree from him and reshaped it even more radically. Jesus probably knew a form of the Ahikar fable. But he told it in a new way, which made it a counter-story to the Ahikar fable. Jesus' counter-thesis is that there is hope for renewal even for a tree which has looked like a dead trunk for three years. So too with human beings: God gives an opportunity even to someone who has failed to achieve anything for a long time, for whom nothing has been happening for a long time, from whom no fruits and nothing useful are to be expected. Jesus' counter-thesis runs: human beings can change – even if so much pessimistic experiential wisdom tells against this. For even an allegedly dead tree can bring forth fruit again if one digs up the garden and puts manure on the soil. It is not that we find a naive optimism about the possibility of change in the preaching of Jesus, from which after centuries we perhaps turn away pessimistically because human beings have not changed. Quite the contrary: Jesus' parable of the fig tree presupposes a centuries-old pessimism of the kind that has found its way into the wisdom traditions of the ancient East – and contradicts it.

What I learned during my study is still valid: as Christians we are obliged to hold fast to the message that human beings are capable of change, are capable of repentance, and to put it forward against widespread pessimism. Human beings can change, even if they sometimes look as unchangeable as a dead piece of wood. Human beings can overcome war, xenophobia and oppression. They can take small steps in this direction, and each step is a step into the kingdom of God.

Looking back on my existentialist phase, I would say that at that time I found questionable the hope expressed by Mark's parable of the fig tree, the hope for a great change in the world. At that time it seemed to me to be mythology. But I found an answer in Luke's parable of the fig tree. This was that though the possibility of great change in the world may be questionable, it is possible for the individual to change – even though sometimes one may doubt it.

The second phase of my thinking was connected with the 1968 rebellion. That came at the end of my studies. It brought more than the throwing of eggs and tomatoes and other missiles, which my generation allowed itself at that time. It brought a new political awareness. And for many people at the time that was an illumination. At that time we discovered in Luke's parable of the fig tree a new answer to the question 'How is it possible for a person to change?' The change takes place in the parable not directly through the transformation of the tree, say by pruning it, cutting off old branches, but through the transformation of the surroundings, changing the vineyard.

Anyone familiar with biblical imagery will know that the vineyard is a stereotype for the whole people of Israel, i.e. for the whole society in which the individual is rooted. One only has to think of Isaiah's parable of the vineyard (Isa.5.1ff.) or the Gospel parable of the workers in the vineyard (Mark 12.1ff. par.). In speaking of a transformation of the whole vineyard the parable says that individuals have a chance if something changes throughout the society in which they are rooted. For individuals to change, structures must change. That was the political awareness which dawned on many people with the student rebellion – and which we cannot go back on, even after the excesses and aberrations of that rebellion. Whereas existentialist theology said, 'The individual must and may change, that is the great turning point', the new theology of political awareness said, 'It's not enough to call on the individual to change; society must change.' The images of a great change involving the whole world now no longer seemed to be old-fashioned mythology. One recognized a truth in them, but in pictorial form: that the transformation of the individual is connected with the great transformation of the world. I began to rediscover something of the truth of Mark's parable of the fig tree.

However, of course this new theology of political awareness also had a great problem: how can one produce a consensus among Christians where political responsibility is involved? For there are very different ideas and dreams about the political shape of society: black, blue-and-yellow, red, and green dreams. And it would be a bad thing if there were not this variety of dreams among us. But because of that there are inevitably disputes in the churches.

We mustn't become resigned because of this dispute. In my view it's possible to arrive at a consensus over some points, at least over what we reject. Let me demonstrate that by Mark's parable of the fig tree.

At the end of this parable we find the rather enigmatic remark, 'When you see *these things* happening, you know that summer is right at the door.' In the parable *these things* refers to the budding of the fig tree. But in the context of Mark's Gospel they are more. In the previous chapter Jesus speaks about the events of the end. There we read, 'When you see the abomination that causes desolation standing where it does not belong – let the reader understand – then let those who are in Judea flee to the mountains.' For then, the text tells us, a great catastrophe will happen. We now know what the 'abomination that causes desolation' is. This is an allusion to the attempt to desecrate the temple ten years after Jesus' death, when the Roman emperor Gaius Caligula wanted to have his statue set up in the Jerusalem temple, to have himself worshipped there as god. He was murdered before he could carry out his plan. But the anxiety remained that another emperor might carry out this crazy plan and put himself in the place of God. This anxiety was alive when the evangelist wrote his Gospel. And now he is saying to his community: when that happens, when an emperor puts himself on God's throne, then the great catastrophe will come. Then the world will collapse.

Let me express what he says as we would put it. When state and politics usurp the place of God, there is a condition of red alert for

Christians, indeed for all people. Then the world really does threaten to collapse. Politicians want only put themselves in God's place when they lay down conditions on which they are ready to destroy the world by a nuclear suicide. Or when they want to decide what life deserves to live and what does not. For then they are taking the place of the one who alone is Lord over life and death. Then they are acting like those Roman emperors who want to be worshipped in the temple as god. Then they are overstepping their limits as human beings. And I am certain that all Christians reject this. I am certain that all Christians agree when I say, 'No state, no politician, no institution (not even the church) may take the place of God.' I believe that there is a negative consensus here, a consensus over what we reject.

But more positive consensus is possible than we often think. Let me mention just two attitudes to the basic dimensions of social life: the relationship between in-groups and outsiders and the relationship between above and below. Here there are very clear tendencies in the Bible.

The first tendency says: outsiders and strangers are to be treated as members of one's own group. Even enemies are creatures loved by God. Every stranger is the image of God. For me, one of the most positive experiences in our churches is the way in which they resist the popular trend towards xenophobia. That's not something to take for granted. It doesn't make for popularity everywhere.

The second tendency relates to the relationship between superiors and subordinates, above and below. Here too the Bible says clearly: anyone who wants to be first should be prepared to take on the role of someone who is right at the bottom. Rule is no longer to be taken for granted. It becomes a problem. There will always be a dispute over the consequences of this – but the fact that rule becomes a problem is something that should unite us all.

For that reason I hope that theology will never again lose its political awareness. But this would have to be a theology which also assimilates those disappointments experienced by the rebellious generation of 1968. Some of the erstwhile rebels became resigned and withdrew into a private sphere. Theology, too, is always in danger of losing its political awareness and withdrawing into questions of personal life. That would be fatal in a world in which there are so very many public tasks.

But how are we to prevent our concern to cultivate the whole vineyard from being paralysed? How are we to avoid succumbing to the illusion that it is enough for us to work a small private corner in it – and then all will be well? Such questions led to a third phase of reflection in the 1980s. And in it I read the parables of the fig tree yet again. The parable in Mark does not in fact say 'Change the world', but 'Look for signs that the world is changing.' The world is changing without your having anything to do with it. You just have to learn from nature: as the supposedly dead and dried-up fig tree puts out leaves, so too green keeps sprouting in our asphalt world and shows that we are not yet completely dead. But where are we to discover such signs of hope in nature, which are independent of our successes and failures?

Sometimes one hits on new ideas by chance, and that was the case here. While I was teaching German and religion in a school, I once caught a pupil reading a book on a different subject under his desk. It was a book on evolution and evolutionary theory. The pupil said to me with shining eyes, 'It's very interesting.' He told me that I should read it instead of grumbling about finding him out. I wrote down the title and bought the book. The pupil was absolutely right. It was very interesting, much more interesting than my lesson, even to me as a theologian. If one regards the whole world as a giant evolutionary process in which everything is gradually changing, one can discover signs of the new everywhere. One can then perceive traces of the future even where everything seems to be stagnating. One can see green sprouting up everywhere. One can learn in a new way from the fig tree to heed the signs of the future. That marked the beginning of an 'evolutionary phase' in my thought. I still have many unanswered questions, and there is much that I would like to develop further. But today I would like to stress two insights: first, that the human being is a transition, and second, that the human being is an adaptation to an unknown reality.

I believe that human beings are a transitional stage in evolution. They are not finished and complete. We are still in the midst of this transition. Nowadays it is usually taken for granted that we are part of biological evolution. At least, I never had any difficulty in accepting that animals are our brothers and sisters. But at the same time it is equally indisputable that there is a great gap between animals and human beings. So scientists keep looking for the missing link between primates and man. But perhaps we already know all this all too well. Perhaps we ourselves are this missing link, i.e. a being still in process of realizing its full humanity, still in the transitional stage between being animal and being human. This thought struck me like a thunderbolt, that we are citizens of two worlds: an old world to which we still belong in all phases of our organic life, and a new world into which we have only just entered. For if we calculate the time since the appearance of life in the cosmos as one day, human beings appeared only just before midnight – quite late. Only with them to some degree did something new begin. In the old world it may be that we are instinctively against all strangers. In the new world that is not the case. In the old world it may be that we make ourselves dependent through rule. In the new world that is not the case. In the old world it may be a matter of course that we kill each other in wars. In the new we do not.

The New Testament bears witness to this new world; indeed the whole of the New Testament is steeped in the conviction that we are at the crossroads between two worlds, that the old world is coming to an end and a new one is already beginning in secret now. The whole of the New Testament says, 'The time is fulfilled, the kingdom of God is at hand. Repent and believe in the gospel.' Is it perhaps right in a very simple sense? Did not something of this new world appear in Jesus? A world which does not run by the rules of 'eat or be eaten'? A world in which the outsiders are part of ourselves? A world in which the privileged are ready to take the lowliest positions? The New Testament bears witness to a transition of cosmic dimensions which is independent of the success and failure of individual human dreams, even independent of whether the dreams of the student rebellion of 1968 were fulfilled or not.

You may say, 'But that's speculation!' An American colleague recently asked me, 'Do you really believe that something essential will change in human evolution in the next 200 years?' I was perplexed, and resorted to the answer in II Peter, that for God a thousand years are as a day – and that by evolutionary standards this span is still far too short. But that wasn't a satisfactory answer.

Now I know what I should have told him. Now I would say, 'If in fact human beings are still living on this earth in two hundred years, and if by then we haven't turned the earth into a poisoned pile of rubble, then something essential will have changed in us human beings. In that case we would have achieved something unprecedented: we would have refrained from unleashing the destructive powers we have at our disposal. Indeed we would have taken a powerful step towards the new human being if our successors could meet again for a Kirchentag in Berlin in two hundred years time.' Hope for that is a great sign, one of the signs that we can learn from the fig tree.

And now, to end with, my second thought. Human beings are adaptations to an unknown reality. All life is an adaptation to the overall system of reality. In an infinite process of trial and error, stable configurations of matter develop, some capable of reduplication and even of intensifying their internal order. That same overall system of reality makes this process possible, has produced us and all things, sustains us, and judges us by preserving only what ultimately corresponds to it. It is no false humility when I say that we are absolutely dependent on this overall system of reality down to the last phases of our bodies. But we have a special place. All things suffer this adaptation to what holds reality together in its innermost realm dumbly. Only we, human beings, experience it consciously, as a task, as an obligation – and also as a gift. As the representatives of all creatures we may consciously lead our lives as a response to reality as a whole – and for Christian faith the ultimate reality is God himself, the mystery of reality that will never be wholly accessible to us. While biological evolution progresses by eliminating the incompatible and the unadapted, this ultimate reality has disclosed itself to us in the New Testament in quite a different way. It does not exclude what has failed, what has not adapted; it gives it a chance. It gives the shrivelled-up tree a chance to live – although it really should be dug up. Really there should be selection here. It should be felled, removed, burned. But God gives an opportunity for repentance. The parable of the barren fig tree thus contains a protest against what has determined the whole of biological evolution so far: a protest against the selection of the incompatible, the unadapted, the useless – indeed a protest against the principle of selection itself. And in so doing it points to a new phase of evolution into which we have entered, a world in which there is life which does not live at the expense of other life.

My starting point was that the New Testament bears witness to a disappointed hope. That's true. Men and women at that time expected the breaking in of a new, wonderful world in their time. This expectation was a mistake. But this mistake is the reverse of a truth which dawned at that time: that we are living in a transitional stage between an old world and a new one. Anyone who recognizes that and repents has already entered this new world, has become the citizen of a new world.

Anyone on whom that has dawned hopes for a change in human beings and the world, a hope which can be burdened by many disappointments – including the disappointment that Christianity and the church have 'improved' human beings and the world so little.

For anyone on whom that hope has dawned, a great light has entered life between birth and death, for in each of us this transition into a new world is constantly taking place afresh.

Anyone on whom that hope has dawned knows that we take steps towards this new world wherever, by political action, we are concerned for a humane society in which no human being exercises the power which only belongs to God – but also where no fallible human being is required to have capacities which only God can have.

Whatever we do, in private and in public life, will only be trial and error, a hypothesis with which we attempt to correspond to God. Anyone whom this prospect of trial and error saddens may learn from the fig tree that God continually gives us a chance to repent, even if we look as dead as a withered tree. And God continually gives us signs of hope that the world will change – no matter how dead and withered that world may seem.

The Open Door to Life
A penitential sermon

(Luke 13.23-30)

*Someone asked him, 'Lord, are only a few people going to be saved?'
He said to them, 'Make every effort to enter through the narrow door,
because many, I tell you, will try to enter and will not be able to. Once
the owner of the house gets up and closes the door, you will stand
outside knocking and pleading, "Sir, open the door for us." But he
will answer, "I don't know where you come from." Then you will say,
"We ate and drank with you, and you taught in our streets." But he
will reply, "I don't know where you come from. Away from me, you
evildoers!" There will be weeping there, and gnashing of teeth, when
you see Abraham, Isaac and Jacob and all the prophets in the kingdom
of God, but you yourselves thrown out. People will come from east
and west and north and south, and will take their places at the feast in
the kingdom of God. Indeed there are those who are last who will be
first, and first who will be last.'*

In earliest Christianity there must have been people with nightmares.
Our text shows it: it contains the nightmare of useless knocking on
the door, a double nightmare.

First of all there is the nightmare of the many and the few. Many
want to get in through the door, but only a few have an opportunity.
Many pursue the goal, but only a few reach it.

Then there is the second nightmare of the first and the last: the
many who are excluded not only have to see how very few are
admitted. They also have to put up with looking on from afar while
hosts of people stream past them to the goal from which they are
excluded.

There is no logical connection between the two images: the image
of the narrow door which makes entry into the kingdom of heaven

difficult, and the picture of people streaming from afar, from all points of the compass, which gives the impression that there are no longer any doors to the kingdom of heaven, as though it had open frontiers. Dreams aren't logical. A nightmare of final failure leads to wailing and gnashing of teeth, but no coherent thought-processes.

I ought to go on to say a good deal about the significance of such mythical images of the Last Judgment, and do a good deal of demythologizing here. Fortunately, however, the image of useless knocking on the gates of heaven is still alive today – in jokes. There is a whole series of jokes about knocking on the gates of heaven, and no one finds it difficult to see what they're all about – even without demythologizing. Here's an example, but not to make you laugh. It's no laughing matter, and in any case it's dated.

Erich Honecker knocks on the heavenly door. Peter opens it and inspects the new candidate for the heavenly kingdom. However, he rejects him and sends him to the hell where he belongs. Very soon afterwards there is more loud knocking and a commotion at the gates. Peter looks out. All the devils from the most senior to the most junior are beating on the gates of heaven with their fists in panic. 'Are you crazy?' shouts Peter. 'Get back to hell immediately.' 'No,' cry all the devils in agitation, 'We're coming here. We're refugees and ask for asylum. You've sent us someone who wants to turn hell into a "place of heavenly peace". That's too much, even for us poor devils, so we're running away.'

In East Germany such jokes are sharp weapons. But we find that they leave a bad taste in the mouth. West Germans see their country as the heaven into which many refugees stream. They see themselves in the role of Peter who examines them rather than as those under scrutiny – and as for the many poor devils who stream in not only from the East but from other points of the compass...

So we need to try some variations on this story of knocking on the gates of heaven. Here are three possible ones.

First, a group from West Germany arrives at the heavenly gates. Above them is written 'Entrance to the Democratic Heaven'. Peter opens up – he looks like a cross between Thomas Jefferson and George Washington. The candidates are tested. Peter says 'I don't know you', but they protest, 'You know us very well. We've lived for forty years in a modern spirit, in a model democracy, with a model constitution.' But Peter shakes his head. 'We don't recognize your model democracy in heaven. You didn't achieve it, fight for it. It was given from above. You had to buy widespread public assent to it with the economic miracle. And you've often legitimated it by looking down on your neighbours in the East and saying, "Lord, how good it is that we don't live like those people there." So you've become self-satisfied, rich and fat. While your elites got involved in a chain of scandals, you watched unperturbed as your society broke solidarity with the losers. You'll get a surprise! You will weep and gnash your teeth as the East Germans go past you and are admitted. They've doggedly struggled for the beginning of a new democracy. They've begun, perhaps for the first time in German history, to build a democracy from below. They are the ones far off who now are near. And they will stream in – and with them Russians, Poles and Hungarians – and be accepted. But as far as you are concerned – Away with you, hypocrites. You do not correspond to the model of democracy that we have in heaven.'

In our favour, I asume that Peter will not send us straight to hell, but to the purgatory of democratic purification, with the task of reflecting on his words especially on days of penitence and prayer.

Some of the group refuse to be sent away. They argue: 'We're Christians. We were involved in bringing about a change in East Germany. The dream of freedom hibernated in the churches – in empty, often ruined and neglected churches. It was borne forth from there.' These Christians refuse to be sent away. But Peter shakes his head and says, 'Look elsewhere – perhaps one door along.'

That leads to the second variation on our story. A small group of Christians leaves the host of the rejected at the entrance to the heaven of the religions. They knock. Abraham opens, looks at the newcomers and shakes his head. 'I don't know you.' But the Christians say: 'You know us. You're our father Abraham. We're your children. We have the promise that we will eat with you, Isaac and Jacob in the kingdom of heaven.' Abraham repeats: 'I don't know you. You're not my children. You persecuted and oppressed my children for centuries. By your example you demonstrated that things can't go well with those who don't share your faith – to punish them and endorse yourselves. Over the course of the centuries you've got so used to the idea that things have to go badly with my children that you watched, tolerated and even approved the way in which they were deprived of their rights, deported and murdered. Now you want to come and eat with me in the kingdom of God. Can't you see that that's impossible? That it's cynical – especially as long as many of your theologians are convinced that my children have to remain outside. Depart from me, you hypocrites and evildoers! You don't match the image that heaven has of its children.'

That, too, is an appropriate thought for days of penitence and prayer. Beyond question a good deal still has to happen before we can speak with a good conscience – along with Jews and Muslims – of 'our father Abraham'. We're only at the beginning. Let's have no illusions about that.

One from the group of the rejected will not give up. He's a solitary, and looks like Søren Kierkegaard or Franz Kafka. He goes to the nearest gate of heaven and tries once again. The inscription over the gate says, 'This is the entry to the law.'

Before the law stands a doorkeeper. Our man comes up to this doorkeeper and asks to enter. But the doorkeeper says that he cannot be admitted now. The man ponders, and asks whether he may be allowed to enter later. 'It's possible,' says the doorkeeper, 'but not now.' As the door to the law is still open and the doorkeeper has stepped aside, the man tries to look inside through the gate. When the doorkeeper notices this he laughs and says: 'If it so attracts you, try to get in despite my prohibition. But note that I'm powerful, and I'm only the lowliest doorkeeper.' Our man allows himself to be intimidated and decides that he would prefer to wait until he has permission to come in. To make his waiting easier the doorkeeper gives him a stool. He sits on it for days and years. He becomes old and sick. His sight leaves him. But now he can recognize in the darkness a brilliance breaking forth unquenchably from the doors of the law. Before his death he asks the doorkeeper a last question: 'All strive after the law,' the man says. 'How comes it that in these many years no one but me has asked to be admitted?' The doorkeeper recognizes that the man is already at his last gasp, and to get through to his failing hearing he shouts at him: 'No one else

could gain entry here. This entrance was meant only for you. Now
I'm going to shut it.'

This famous parable of the doorkeeper, which I've abbreviated,
expresses the worst nightmare of life: the nightmare of failing
oneself. We don't just want to live up to the image that others have
of a good person or a good democrat. We don't just want to live up
to what can be expected of a Christian generally. We want to find
ourselves. We want to find a door to the life which is there for us;
the one task which only we can perform, the one opportunity which
is meant only for us.

No one will tell us where this door is open. No one can formulate
this task for us. No one can say to us for certain, 'That's your way.'
There are no signposts. And the advice we hear from other people
often leads us astray. We often have to disregard it, act against it,
if we want to live up to the only image that matches us – one which
we do not even know.

It is as though this image were hidden somewhere in the depths
of the world and life, we know not where. We don't know what it
looks like. We don't even know ourselves. And once the door opens,
once a light falls on us from that image, when we're near enough to
grasp it, then perhaps we don't recognize it as our own image.
Perhaps then we don't recognize the way to it as our way – and the
door to it as our door; nor the law as the law that applies to us and
only to us: as a task and opportunity for life, an opportunity which
is given us only once, only between cradle and grave.

Each of us might correspond to this hidden image of themselves.
And each is afraid that he or she will never see it face to face.

Here are some more harmless examples. As children we tried to
live up to the image which our parents had formed of us, just as
pupils try to match the images of teachers, and teachers the image
that pupils carry round of them. Patients turn into the image the
therapist has of them, and sometimes that's helpful. In marriage we
want to match the image our partner has of us. We all have a longing
to live up to the image that others have of us – especially if the others
love us, have a good opinion of us, and we trust them.

But I don't want to talk about all these images now, the images
that others have of us as children, pupils, teachers, partners,
democrats and Christians. I want to talk about that hidden picture

that means something in us that only we ourselves are. Who carries around this picture of us? Whose expectations are we up against here? Or at its heart does life reach into a vacuum? Is there perhaps a gaping nothingness behind the images that others have of us – if we drop out of all these images? Even if one day we found the gate to true life – to ourselves – might we not perhaps be terrified if we opened it, because there was a gruesome solitude behind it? Because it led into a deep night? Because then we would be all alone by ourselves and have to fill this vacuum alone?

How many people are desperate because this image is unattainable in the darkness of life and they suspect that it could be terrible to come upon it? How many people get trapped in addiction and dependence, in order to deafen their awareness that they are far from themselves? How many partnerships break up because they are torn by the anxiety that one might be missing real life, a true life that must lie somewhere else? How many rituals are built up to protect people from anxiety about not doing justice to the hidden picture of themselves? How many depressions are triggered because all the gates to life seem shut – because people think that only others are streaming to the banquet of life, and they are standing outside, where frustration puts them with the hypocrites and those who gnash their teeth? Last but not least, how much spinelessness is the result of desperate self-surrender, with the thought, 'If we're already so far from ourselves, then let's betray the hidden image of ourselves completely.' How much oppression, contempt and injustice becomes possible only through such betrayal!

Indeed if we go in search of that hidden image of ourselves, of that door which is meant for us, then we find ourselves in a wilderness, in a nothingness. But precisely at that point we then find the power which alone creates out of nothingness and can deliver from nothingness: God. The hidden image of ourselves which we seek is the image that God has of us – and that is more than all the images of parents and teachers, of friends and loved ones, of therapists and pastors. To correspond to God's image of us is the secret desire of our life. We are all on the way there.

If on our way we come to the gate of life and knock on it, to join in the feast of life, and the Lord says to us, 'I don't know you,' what do we say to him?

We should say, 'You know us. We bear God's image. God knows his image.'

But what if the Lord says a second time (as in our text), 'I don't know you'?

'I don't recognize God's image in you, since you let corruption become a habit in one of the richest societies in the world and often grossly exploit the weak.

I don't recognize God's image in you when as Christians you want to deny that others are in the true image of God.

I don't recognize God's image in you when you destroy your lives in self-injury and self-abandonment, in spinelessness and dependence.'

When you hear that, you shouldn't give up on the threshold of life, at the gate of the law which is open for you. Say, rather:

'Lord, I see that I can't persuade you to open the gate of life for me. Perhaps my place is rightly outside, before the gate. But if I can't come to you, at least you can come to me. If I can't open the gate of life, at least I can open the gate of my heart to you and let you in. If I can't get through to the law which is to give me life, you can bring it near to me: in the form of the gospel, so that I recognize my image in it as in a mirror.

You yourself brought this remarkable story into the world by entering our lives – in Palestine a long time ago and in difficult circumstances. It was impossible to recognize that you are God's image. But through this story you have shown that the image of God is an indelible seal and remains indelible even when it is damaged by failure and guilt, when grievously it ends in pain and the anguish of death. At that time you yourself were excluded. At that time you suffered before the gates. At that time you were outside, where I am now.

So now I dare invite you to me out here. So I open the gate of my heart to you in order that through you I may be changed into that hidden image that God has formed of me. In order that I, we, may all become children of God.'

What will the Lord do?

He will accept the invitation. He will say to you, 'I love you.' And he will continue with words which we read in the Revelation of John:

Those whom I love, I rebuke and discipline.
So be earnest and repent.
Here I am! I stand at the door and knock.
If anyone hears my voice and opens the door,
I will come in to him and eat with him,
and he with me.

As long as *we* knock at the door of life, we shall always be uncertain whether it will open and we shall be admitted. But if there is knocking at our door, then it is up to us whether we admit the one who wants to enter, and whether we celebrate the feast of life with him.

If we admit Jesus, if we really live in his Spirit, we don't belong to the anti-democratic obscurantists. To live in his spirit means that the first is ready to take the place of the last. That's not yet democracy, which calls for organs, institutions, controls – but all these organs quickly become overpowering structures of domination unless there is something of this Spirit in them.

If we admit Jesus, then we need have no anxiety about being caught up in the pernicious anti-Jewish traditions of our Christianity and our whole culture. Jesus is a Jew. One cannot love him without loving his whole world, the world of Judaism. When Jesus is played off against Judaism, something goes wrong – historically, but perhaps also in human and theological terms. It's as though one married a woman and said to her: 'But I don't want your parents, your brothers and sisters, your nephews and nieces.'

But above all, if we let Jesus into our lives, then we will be rid of the dark nightmare of life. Then we will no longer be terrified by the nothingness into which our life is cast between cradle and grave. We will be secure in the power which creates from nothing. Then the gates of life will open and we shall feel a bond with all people – in north and south, east and west; with all people in whom the same longing for life is awake as is in us. And the door will stand open.

So may the peace of God, which passes all our understanding, keep your hearts and minds in Christ Jesus. Amen.

The Lost Sheep
Or, God's remarkable mathematics

(Luke 15.3-7)

Then Jesus told them this parable: 'Suppose one of you has a hundred sheep and loses one of them. Does he not leave the ninety-nine in the open country and go after the lost sheep until he finds it? And when he finds it, he joyfully puts it on his shoulders and goes home. Then he calls his friends and neighbours together and says, "Rejoice with me; I have found my lost sheep." I tell you that in the same way there wil be more rejoicing in heaven over one sinner who repents than over ninety-nine righteous persons who do not need to repent.'

The shepherd abandons ninety-nine sheep to save one lost sheep. Even as a child that irritated me. 'What happened to the ninety-nine sheep?' I asked myself. 'Who looked after them? Who saw that they didn't stray? That the wolf didn't come and eat them?' Does 99 = 1 in God's mathematics? Are ninety-nine sheep worth as much as one sheep? That could be possible. Why shouldn't God make such equations, since a thousand years for him are as a day?

Nowadays I would use this example to explain God's mathematics to a child. There's a small kingdom in Europe. When you cross its frontiers with a car you're given a little folder. It says: 'Our kingdom is very small. We can't spare any of our inhabitants. So we've introduced strict speed limits on motorways and roads.' This small country has understood God's mathematics well. It has understood better than we have that if only one less person came to grief there would be justification for causing inconvenience to all the rest. The one person saved is worth a change in the lives and conduct of everyone else. And what do people say here? I often get the impression that for many people in our country dying trees would be a stronger argument for changing our highway code than dying people. Our country needs a lot more teaching before it understands God's mathematics.

We all need lessons. As a child I hesitated over one lost sheep being worth more than ninety-nine good sheep: as a grown-up I had other difficulties with these figures. Is it really true that there is one lost sheep for every ninety-nine righteous? Isn't that unrealistic? Isn't the opposite the case, that there are ninety-nine scoundrels for every just person and ninety-nine lost sheep for every one saved? Indeed there are so many lost sheep that one can't mention them all. However, here are just a few portraits.

There is the *abandoned* sheep. Let's hear its complaint. It says: 'Even as a child I was often left alone. My parents were away. I longed for them to come. But there was no way I could get them. I wondered whether they would ever come.' There are many such lost sheep among us. All their lives they keep waiting for someone to come to them like a father or mother, for someone to hold them in their arms and say again that all is well. Inwardly they've remained small children, children who feel helpless to get others to come to them in any way, children who can only imagine that the other – the partner who understands everything – will be there as inexplicably as their parents always were in childhood. There are many sheep with this 'abandonment syndrome', as the psychologists call it. What shall we say to them? The parable gives some indication. The longing for the 'good shepherd' who comes to you and takes you on his shoulder, to whom you can cling – all that is contained in it. But the parable doesn't stop there. It talks of 'repentance'. In heaven there is joy over one lost one who repents, one who actually changes direction, one who doesn't just wait passively to be fetched, one who comes to realize, 'I'm not abandoned. I can change my life. I can, I may, repent. Then I shall find the good shepherd.'

There is a second kind of lost sheep. This is the *misunderstood*, the embittered sheep. These are often very original sheep. They've dared to graze apart from the flock. They've gone on to new ground, but not so far away from the flock that they can't be seen. Indeed, whenever they had a good idea they sneaked a look at the flock – to see whether someone might have noticed how good their idea was. They longed for admiration and recognition. But the flock grazed peacefully on. And sometimes even bleated in a way that in unfavourable acoustics sounded like the mocking bleating of goats. The misunderstood sheep say to themselves, 'This flock is stupid, short-sighted, conceited, envious.' And yet they long for recognition by this stupid, short-sighted, conceited and envious flock. They want to be caressed by those whom they want to despise from the bottom of their hearts. Indeed what they would like best would be to return to the flock. But they're afraid that once again there would be mocking bleating: 'So at last you've come to your right mind! You've finally realized that you're nothing special.' As a result they suffer from emotional self-poisoning, which draws them more and more deeply into their own hurt. What can we say to them? For them too the parable has something to say: it speaks of the joy of conversion. Joy about others – not *Schadenfreude*, but simple joy that someone has come back. If we could make something of this joy accessible to all the embittered, hurt and misunderstood sheep, perhaps they would repent! Indeed, could the flock emanate something of this joy – or is it a joy which can exist only in heaven, which isn't on earth? I doubt that.

Now to the third kind of 'lost sheep', the *depraved* sheep. It's really disquieting that we meet so many of these depraved sheep nowadays. They're sheep which remain in the flock and pursue the same aims as the rest of the sheep, but do so by breaking the rules. As they agree with everyone else on their aims, they're furious when their practices are described as what they are – an expression of depravity. This depravity can begin with shoplifting, is practised as a harmless sport and trivialized – and extends to the uppermost levels of society. We all think it a good thing for people to use their activity and energy in government. But that doesn't justify their looking after their own interests as well. We all think that the creation of new jobs by entrepreneurial activity is a good thing – but that's no justification for poisoning the environment. These lost sheep often don't understand why they're criticized. Even when they've been convicted of their transgressions, they act as though they would enjoy their environment only in 'sunshine' – and not poisoned with lead. What are we to say to these depraved sheep? There's also something in the parable for them. There is more joy among us and in heaven when one of them repents – and quickly resigns – than over the ninety-nine self-righteous who cannot be taught. Let me be quite blunt about this: the clarity with which now and again some sheep formerly involved in the stench of depravity draw the consequences is a comfort, a ray of light. We should all rejoice at it!

Someone might ask, 'But aren't there also some good sheep among all the lost, all the forsaken, embittered and depraved sheep? Indeed aren't there a great many good sheep?' Of course there are. But they too are poor sheep: they are sheep of whom too much is asked. It isn't just the actual amount of work. People can achieve an amazing amount! Work gets too much where it isn't recognized. The good sheep get into difficulties justifying their very dull existence in a situation in which you're regarded as a failure if you aren't out of the ordinary – even if this is as a result of being forsaken, misunderstood or depraved; in which it is a fault to do routine things well, competently and reliably, and to cope respectably with everyday matters.

What follows from all this? It is our average experience that not only one lost sheep equals ninety-nine others, but ninety-nine sheep equal an enigmatic sheep which has not yet been found!

My next question is, 'Why are so many lost? Why are so many forsaken, misunderstood, depraved?' Isn't it because all the sheep have lost their direction and support? Haven't they all lost the confidence that we are never finally forsaken in this life, never wholly misunderstood? Haven't they forgotten that there are criteria which cannot be formulated at will for domestic use, by which we can measure ourselves even when we are all alone. In short, that life is a gift and a task? We haven't even given it to ourselves. We haven't even given ourselves the task of living. And because we no longer know and experience that, we're ninety-nine lost sheep – and look for the one which wasn't lost and remained unknown.

Now comes the last step in my attempt to explain God's mathematics. Is the parable really about a ratio of 99:1? Isn't it about the relationship of one hundred sheep to the one shepherd? Indeed, is it a parable about the lost sheep at all?

If I put myself in the situation of the ninety-nine, I would say that it's a parable of the lost shepherd. One missing sheep wouldn't cause any disturbance in a large flock. Perhaps it wouldn't even be noticed.

But what happens when the shepherd goes? That causes difficulties for the flock.

How does it react? Of course there are sheep who say, 'We ought to find something better than a shepherd, protection that will never disappear. Weren't our ancestors free sheep – without a shepherd, without domestication? Mustn't we have an innate capacity to live without a shepherd (without all the refinement of cultivation and hedges and water troughs)?' In short, there is an outbreak of 'primal sheep romanticism'. The sheep want to return to nature, to snuggle up together as to a great mother. And they have a great longing never to have to run away again.

But that's only one possible answer. I would like to add another, a variation on the story of the flock.

Once upon a time there was a flock of sheep. One day the shepherd disappeared. The sheep became restless. 'Where's the shepherd?' they asked in agitation. One of them said, 'He'll come back. We must just be patient.' Another said, 'He's disappeared for ever, we must get on without him.' A third suggested, 'Perhaps he's looking for a lost sheep.' A fourth said, 'Perhaps something has happened to him.' But a particularly wise sheep said, 'We must look for the shepherd. We must do something to get over this lack of direction. Perhaps the shepherd has only gone away to test us. Perhaps he wants us to behave differently from the way in which sheep usually do.' So they decided to look for the shepherd. They formed small reconnaisance parties and combed the country. They didn't find the shepherd. But they found many lost sheep and brought them all home. They would never have imagined how many sheep were lost. But they never found the shepherd. However, they didn't give up. Finally they came upon him. They were too late. He had fallen among robbers. The sheep saw in helpless rage that the robbers had first plundered and robbed him, and then killed him. Confused and in grief they returned.

But then one of the wise sheep came forward. It had studied theology and had a certain eloquence. It said, 'Do not sorrow, dear fellow sheep. The shepherd is alive!' The sheep listened to him in amazement. 'He's alive?' 'Yes, he's alive. Had he not been lost we would never have found all our lost brothers and sisters. He fell among robbers for all of us. How many owe him their lives? And so he lives on – in all the sheep who were lost and are saved. He lives on in us who seek our lost brothers and sisters. He is close to us when we find them, when we raise up the sick again, when we give the forsaken courage to act, when we put the depraved on the right way. Fellow sheep, you're looking for a direction, for support, for comfort, for a shepherd. There is a clear direction for us. We have to turn to the lost. We've simply to ask ourselves how to arrange our lives and our society in such a way that even the poorest, the handicapped, the sick, the weak, the prisoners, the burnt out, can live with us. How can we live so that the losers are not lost?'

Then another sheep came forward from the flock. It too had studied theology, but at another school. It protested, 'You're distorting the old parable. Why don't you simply speak of the shepherd who returns bringing the lost sheep on his shoulders? It isn't our task to bring back the lost. Who could do that? That's arrogance. Only the shepherd can do that, no one else.'

What are we to reply? Let's listen to the parable. Jesus says, 'And when he finds it, he joyfully puts it on his shoulders.' I keep thinking about this image: the lost sheep on the shepherd's shoulders. And the more I think about it, the closer the two come together. Wherever I see the shepherd I see the lost sheep. Wherever I see a lost sheep I see the shepherd. The two belong very closely together. We can't see, find and experience one without the other. Jesus is simultaneously the good shepherd and the lamb who bears the lostness of the world.

And then the parable continues: 'He goes home. Then he calls his friends and neighbours together and says, "Rejoice with me; I have found my lost sheep." '

That's what I would like to say to everyone, to the sheep who dream of primal sheep romanticism and the sheep who stubbornly want to remain alone, the sheep who have studied theology and the sheep who haven't, the sheep who are liberal and those who think in fundamentalist terms: we all have reasons for joy when we're reunited with our lost brothers and sisters – with the forsaken, the misunderstood, the embittered, the depraved and the overstretched. Believe me, if we focus our life on the lost, our life will have direction and security. There will be much joy – in heaven and on earth. And if we rediscover only one lost sheep we shall sense something of that great joy in our hearts which is identical to the joy of God over his creatures when they return to the truth. And we shall experience that the peace which passes all our understanding will keep our hearts and minds in Christ Jesus. Amen.

Believing and Thanking
On the gift of changing good fortune into gratitude

———

(Luke 17.11-19)

Now on his way to Jerusalem, Jesus travelled along the border between Samaria and Galilee. As he was going into a village, ten men who had leprosy met him. They stood at a distance and called out in a loud voice, 'Jesus, Master, have pity on us!' When he saw them, he said, 'Go, show yourselves to the priests.' And as they went, they were cleansed. One of them, when he saw he was healed, came back, praising God in a loud voice. He threw himself at Jesus' feet and thanked him – and he was a Samaritan. Jesus asked, 'Were not all ten cleansed? Where are the other nine? Was no one found to return and give rise to God except this foreigner?' Then he said to him, 'Rise and go; your faith has made you well.'

Believing is the gift of changing good fortune into gratitude to God. The story of the ten lepers tells of this gift. These ten have amazing good fortune. They are healed and restored to life. Whereas previously they had had to keep away from other people, now they may return to their homes, their families, to the protective routines of everyday life. But only one of them turns this good fortune into gratitude. Only one returns to Jesus, an outsider of outsiders, a Samaritan.

The story was told so that we should put ourselves on the side of this one person. But we more naturally find ourselves with the nine others. We find it difficult to transform good fortune into gratitude, even this morning. Everyone in this church has had the good fortune to wake up again every morning so far – otherwise none of us would be sitting here. But I know that some people are not grateful for this. Some feel homeless in their own lives, banished from them like lepers from their village. Some people are thinking of those who

94

were seriously injured at Ramstein, hovering between death and life. And after our collection for Amnesty International, scenes of imprisonment and torture will be going through some people's heads. That's perhaps a motivation for giving generously. But not for praise and thanksgiving. Doesn't the story of the ten lepers reflect our inner state? In ninety per cent of our lives we are a long way from praise and thanksgiving. Ninety per cent in us, sometimes a hundred per cent, is dumb. Let's allow this ninety per cent a word. Let's allow it to break its silence. Then we shall try to say why we nevertheless give thanks and praise.

Let's imagine that we ask one of those who have been healed why he didn't go back. I imagine that he would say: 'On my way back to my village healed, I passed lepers whom no one had healed. I was ashamed of myself. My good fortune became a burden. Wasn't my good fortune injustice compared with the misfortune of the others? Didn't they have the same right to life as I did? How can I give thanks if God arbitrarily overwhelms one person with good fortune and makes someone else sit in the dark? I don't feel like saying thank-you but more like complaining, crying out, protesting.'

What should we say to him?

We should invite him to protest with us. For those who cannot protest with all their hearts cannot give thanks. Common to protest and thanksgiving is that they are both infinite affirmations of life. If we protest about the victims of Ramstein it is because it is wanton to risk human lives for a questionable piece of aerobatics. It is wanton because it shows contempt for the infinite value of each individual life. This value makes us protest when life is threatened, when it is overwhelmed, when it is destroyed. And it makes us give thanks when it is saved, becomes secure and free. Those who want to give thanks and praise must learn to protest – must learn to cry out against misfortune and injustice.

Let's ask someone else in our imagination why he did not go back. Perhaps he will say: 'The healing was programmed into the course of things, it was regular. Everyone was affected, not just me. Perhaps we had the same virus which exhausted itself in each of us in comparable circumstances. In no way is there a personal power behind all this which has a purpose for us. There is no need for thanks.'

What do we say to this sceptic?

We should concede that he is right on one point. There is in fact no need to give thanks. Thanks must be voluntary. The less the purpose behind thanksgiving (say a belief that gratitude strengthens the immune system and so will ward off viruses in the future), the more authentic thanksgiving is. Thanksgiving is voluntary and spontaneous and cannot be produced by arguments, however good. And the same goes for protest. Of course when an accident happens one can say, 'There was a mistake over the flight path. A safety system failed. The whole thing was a technical error.' But where is there protest here? Involvement? Indignation? Those who can no longer thank will soon no longer be able to protest.

Let's ask a third one of those who didn't return. Perhaps he will say, 'I couldn't forget the misery of these last years – above all the religious discrimination against us as lepers. Religious tabus made our suffering worse. Dependence on them was hostile to life. For me the way to a new life is a departure from all religions – from the established religion of the priests, but also from the alternative religion of that itinerant guru who advised us to go to the priest.'

What do we say to him?

If we have seen how the fate of Aids victims is sometimes made worse by moral and religious ideas, we can accept the argument. For moralists feel this an occasion for letting loose their sublime aggression against others. But Jesus does not endorse such discrimination; he deliberately scorned religious tabus when people suffered under them. However, the argument of our religious critic goes further: in principle gratitude is often suspected of being reactionary. Thanksgiving is reaction to something that we have not done ourselves. So does gratitude encourage readiness to accept what is given? Doesn't religious belief above all help us to accept the fortuitous and the inexplicable, that irreducible remnant which no rational organization can remove? We are assured of that at least by sociologists and philosophers who are well-disposed towards religion: the task of religion is coping with contingency. One could agree if it became clear that any prayer which accepts life as a wonderful gift of God removes this life from human control and the omnipotence of society so that no authority, no administration, no scientific elite has the right to control it. Our faith is little suited to relieving society of cares about the remaining problems of life. On the contrary, if life is to be completely controlled, then those who experience their lives as a miracle will be the last free people. They will become grit in the machine. They evade external direction precisely by recognizing an absolute dependence on the irreversible conditions of life and turn it into thanksgiving and protest, a dependence which makes them free from all earthly authorities, a dependence on God.

Lastly let's ask a fourth one of those who did not return. He says quietly that really he would like to say thank-you. But as a leper he has belonged to a small minority for long enough. Now he doesn't want once again to belong to a minority which deviates from the general trend. Now he doesn't want to go with the ten per cent but prefers the ninety per cent.

Beyond question public expression of faith and thanks has become a minority situation. Anyone who deliberately behaves in a 'religious' way can become an outsider in many areas of our society. That's a result of our modern age. But this entailed another development, and our story is almost an example of it: the one who repents is a foreigner, an alien. This reflects a feature of earliest Christianity: it was an international community which permeated the whole world. Here is another parallel to modern Christianity, which has become more ecumenical than ever. While its influence waned in traditionally Christian countries, it spread in other cultural circles. It became the religion which is represented most clearly everywhere – in societies with very different structures, in all continents, in all cultures. So Christianity has a quite special task in bringing the world together.

So what should we say to our ninety per cent of conformists? We should say, 'Yes, that's certainly so. Conscious Christian faith is a matter for a small minority – but this minority is distributed everywhere; it has a special task, a task for everyone, for the whole world.'

The arguments of the four who didn't return shows that it isn't easy to enter into dialogue with God, to change good fortune into thanksgiving and suffering into protest, indeed to lead one's whole life as an answer to God's call. So our basic question is, 'What kind of a dialogue is this? What singles it out? What is special about it?'

I shall try to bring that out by a comparison with another process which has the form of a dialogue. My comparison will be with science – an activity in which many of us are involved.

We also ask questions in science – and if they are intelligent and methodically disciplined questions we are rewarded with answers. The answers in turn lead to future questions. Out of the questions and answers arises a history which also has fortuitous elements – i.e. presuppositions, paradigms and premises which one can only narrate and not justify. Very few scientists could experience this dialogue as dialogue with God. So we read in Heisenberg that at some moments the order of reality disclosed by the natural sciences became as intensely present to him as the person of another human being. Such experiences are limit-experiences, signs which point beyond the scientific process to a dialogue with another structure.

Two things are different in the dialogue with God. In science we ask questions. In faith we find that we are the ones who are asked. We are the ones who have to give an answer, an answer with our whole lives, with thought, feeling and action. We find life a task which we have not given ourselves. We have no control over the conditions in which the experiment of our life is to take place, about the place and time, origin and body to which we are bound all our lives. We can only accept all that – either as chance, as the trivial background to our life, or as a question to us to which only we ourselves can give an answer, in terms of thanksgiving and protest.

And that's the second difference. In science we carry on a dialogue in which we are replaceable. Our questions must be formulated in such a way that anyone else could formulate them – man or woman, European or African, Christian or Muslim. In that dialogue with God, however, things are different. Here we are addressed as irreplaceable persons: as the sons or daughters of these parents and no others, with this history and no other, with a stubby nose, grey hair, neuroses and some talents. In this one life, which does not exist anywhere else – and in this one future death which no one else suffers, the voice of God makes itself heard.

I believe that no one can enter into dialogue with God unless they have first heard this voice in their personal lives. Where are you, Adam? Where are you, Eve?

I think a parable may clarify what I mean. We are like a man who goes skiing in the Alps in winter. He has chosen a place and an area to meet his needs. For him the Alpine landscape is a means of recreation. But while he is standing one morning at the top of a slope covered in virgin snow, he feels an invitation to make a particularly beautiful curve in the snow. It seems that it would be a sin against this landscape if he did anything else. He hears a call in the virgin landscape. He is no longer a means to an end, that of satisfying his needs. It takes him over to fulfil itself.

As I said, this is a parable, a parable of our relationship to reality as a whole. We find ourselves in it, we pursue our ends until we experience a conversion, a powerful call, which moves us to understand our life voluntarily as an answer. No one can demonstrate this conversion. One can only talk about it. It is the same thing as the impossibility of proving that we exist. One can only say, 'It happened like this.' And even that has first to be told us by others. We didn't experience it. It's just the same in the dialogue with God.

Here we are presupposing an old story. The Bible is a fundamental part of this story, a dramatic story between God and human beings, with revolts, protests and desperation – but also with declarations of love, commitments, with praise and thanksgiving. From this story, which others had to tell us before we entered it, we hear more clearly than elsewhere the voice of the one who calls, 'Where are you, Adam? Where are you, Eve?' It is a voice which waits for an answer in thanksgiving and praise without compelling it. We are directed to the story with this voice, because otherwise the dialogue with God breaks off. Otherwise it falls silent in the face of the infinite suffering of the creation and human guilt. For if we give thanks and praise within this story, suffering and guilt are not left out.

Some churches are holding a memorial service today – for the victims of Ramstein. Today of all days the oldest set of lectionary texts provides the story of the grateful Samaritan – a story which is meant to move us to praise and thanksgiving. I considered whether I shouldn't choose another text, one that fitted better. But then I chose it deliberately. For our praise and thanksgiving should not be naive, should continue a long history – a history which also includes the catastrophe of Israel and the cross.

Nevertheless I found it difficult to discover a suitable hymn of praise for this service. I went through the hymn book: 'Praise to the

Lord who all things so wondrously reigneth...', I read. That couldn't
be the hymn. There was no wondrous reign in Ramstein, either in
heaven or on earth. But then I found a hymn of praise – the hymn
that we sang at the beginning – praise of God who forgives our sins,
who accepts our weaknesses, and who goes on to make use of them
even if people play wantonly with aircraft, if they take hostages, if
they torture people. This is praise of a God who is an ally of life
against the powers of death and contempt for human beings.

With such a hymn, even today we can put ourselves alongside the
one Samaritan and give God thanks and praise. Let us give this
Samaritan the last word, just as we listened to the others at the
beginning. Let's ask him, 'Why do you praise God? Why do you
praise him although the others fail to?' Perhaps by way of explanation
he will recount some of the mighty history of praise. Perhaps he will
say:

I praise God on behalf of the others. It's always been like that. It
took millions of years for living beings to develop on this earth.
They were dumb. But a great wisdom emerged in them. They
knew nothing of it. Only human beings changed their silence into
speech. Only they began to praise and thank God. And they did
so on behalf of all creatures.

But not all human beings joined in this praise. Only one people
committed itself to continuing this praise of God. And it held fast
to him even in the greatest catastrophes and abysses of its history,
as it has done to the present day. It praised God on behalf of the
others. It waited patiently for others to take their place beside it.

Starting from this people, men and women gathered in all
nations to continue the dialogue with God. They also include me.
I know that I represent only a minority. But I want to give thanks
and protest on behalf of the many others. Not against them but
for them.

I want to give thanks and protest on behalf of those who feel
excluded, homeless and lepers in their lives.

I want to give thanks and protest on behalf of those who bear
sorrow, but have forgotten how to weep.

I want to give thanks and protest on behalf of those who are overwhelmed with good fortune but cannot turn their good fortune into thanksgiving.

I know that I am not alone here. People like me give thanks and protest in many nations and confessions. I suspect that all religions are fragments of one great dialogue between God and human beings. I sense this dialogue in the limited experiences of science – where the improbable structures of the cosmos suggest a superior reason of which my own reason is only a pale reflection.

So I would like to stand beside the Samaritan whom Jesus moved to give praise and thanks. May this Jesus move your hearts also, so that you can praise and protest. And may his peace which passes all our understanding keep your hearts and minds in God, the Father of our Lord Jesus Christ. Amen.

Where is God?
Five interpretations of 'The kingdom of God is in your midst'

———

(Luke 17.20-21)

One question accompanies us through life – from childhood to old age: Where is God? Where is God so near that we can experience him? That we can say 'God is here!' 'God is there!'

When my oldest son got to the stage of asking questions, he perplexed me with this one. And when I couldn't find an answer, for all my theological knowledge, he answered the question himself. He said, 'You can't see God, but you can see Jesus.' He was thinking of pictures of Jesus. Now he's in senior school. In German lessons he has to write a project on a subject of his own choice. He chose 'God and Science'. And again he raised the old question 'Where is God?' Where is God in the cosmos? Isn't this world a giant system of molecules, elementary particles, fields? Where is God?

In September my second son took part in the great demonstration in the Hunsrück against Cruise missiles. He can't see why we've always only been arming for decades – when at the same time everyone has been asserting that they only want to disarm. He can't see why rich states (like ours) spend enormous sums, enough for us to annihilate one another several times over – while at the same time people are suffering devastating famines. Where is God here? Where is God in history?

Both my sons still often perplex me with their questions. New questions become oppressive. Their grandparents' generation is getting older. Death is getting nearer. Not everyone has the same strong faith as an older relative who had to undergo an operation for cancer two weeks ago and in whose behaviour one could detect the conviction that God is in both life and death. None of us can escape the question, 'Where is God in our personal life?' 'And where is he in dying and death?'

The question 'Where is God?' is an age-old question. Sometimes it is just put in a different way. In Jesus' day people did not so much ask '*Where* is God?' as '*When* will we detect, experience his works? *When* is the kingdom of God coming? *When* will God no longer be hidden in the cosmos, in history, in personal life?' In our text Luke 17.20-21 we read such a question.

Once, having been asked by the Pharisees when the kingdom of God would come, Jesus replied, 'The kingdom of God does not come with your careful observation, nor will people say, "Here it is" or "There it is", because the kingdom of God is in your midst.'

The interpretation of these words of Jesus, 'the kingdom of God is in your midst', is disputed. I don't want to bring in the scholarly dispute for its own sake. Rather, I want to demonstrate that each different interpretation contains a true insight and that in each interpretation there is something that can help us with the question 'Where is God?' 'Where can we experience his activity?' 'Where can I encounter him?' So I shall sketch out five interpretations – as an answer to an age-old question, 'Where is God?'

One widespread interpretation says: Jesus was asked, 'When is the kingdom of God coming?', and he replied, 'God comes so suddenly that he is there among you in a flash, before you can say, "Look, here he is, there he is".' So Jesus was speaking of the future coming of God. This interpretation contains one of the great answers to the question 'Where is God?' It goes: God is now hidden, but one day he will reveal himself. Now we are fumbling in the dark, but one day we shall clearly experience in life and in death that God is there. There are passages in the Bible which point in this direction. But if we begin from our text, that can't be the whole truth. For Jesus doesn't say, 'God's kingdom will one day be in your midst.' He says, 'God's kingdom is in your midst.' God's activity is already there – as hidden as the seed in the earth, which one day will become wheat.

This brings me to another interpretation: Jesus thought that God's kingdom was already beginning in people's hearts. And that brings us to the second great answer to our question 'Where is God?' We look for God outside – in the cosmos and in history. But perhaps he is in us? Perhaps he is in that corner of our innermost being from which come the dreams that in the Bible are sometimes the words of God. Don't we sometimes feel God's working deep within us? Many people nowadays try to take this way inwards. They look for it in meditation on God, seeking to immerse themselves in God. At a very early stage there were Christians who took this course. In the second century after Christ some of them reformulated Jesus' answer. Their version of the saying has been preserved in the Gospel of Thomas. It runs:

> Jesus said, 'If those who lead you say to you, "See, the Kingdom is in the sky", then the birds of the sky will precede you. If they say to you, "It is in the sea", then the fish will precede you. Rather, the kingdom is inside you, and it is outside you. When you come to know yourselves, then you will become known, and you will realize that it is you who are the sons of the living Father. But if you will not know yourselves, you dwell in poverty and it is you who are that poverty.'

To know oneself within, to know that one is related to God in one's innermost being – that is what these Christians saw as the way to God. Why didn't the church include their Gospel in the Bible, although it contained wonderful words of Jesus? The church recognized that anyone can take the way inwards alone. The way inwards is a way to God only when it leads to other people and commits us. That is also presupposed in our text. Jesus does not say, 'The kingdom of God is within your heart', but speaks of a plurality of people among whom the kingdom of God is. He says, 'The kingdom of God is in your midst.' Jesus has a community in mind, not individuals.

That brings me to the third interpretation. Perhaps Jesus meant, 'God's kingdom is at work in your community.' In that case he would almost be repeating another of his sayings, 'Where two or three are gathered together in my name, there I am in the midst of them' (Matt.18.20). This interpretation holds that God's kingdom doesn't just begin in the future, in the individual heart, but in the community – among those who want to follow Jesus and whose lives and hearts have been transformed by him. But – we may ask – isn't that a questionable beginning for the kingdom of God? Did it in fact begin among the disciples who left Jesus in the lurch when he was on the cross – with the exception of those women who proved braver at the decisive moment? And didn't the later disciples of Jesus keep leaving their master in the lurch? Wasn't the church at some periods felt to be more the kingdom of evil than the kingdom of God? If the kingdom of God begins among such questionable people as ourselves, doesn't it then become questionable itself?

That brings me to the fourth interpretation: perhaps Jesus was referring to himself. In him the rule of God is already there. He is in the midst of the disciples. In him they have a criterion for the nearness and presence of God. If we ask 'Where is God?', we can attempt to find God everywhere. For God has the freedom to meet us everywhere: in the world or deep within us, alone or in community, in nature or history. There is no place where God is not present. But only in one place do we have the promise that we will really find him: in Jesus. We are to measure, to test, all experiences in which we sense something of God by him – and part company with whatever is irreconcilable with his message. He is the place where God allows himself to be found. We have no direct access to God. But here he becomes accessible to us. From God a light falls on all other experiences with God.

So far I have presented four interpretations. I wanted to show that we can learn something from the scholarly argument – which is carried on with reference to many dictionaries and many grammars and with the knowledge of many texts. Scholarly interpretation will never lead to completely clear results. Several interpretations often remain possible. But that represents wealth. We can learn from each of them. In search of the one truth we find many little truths, and most of them can help us on our way. It is a well known fact that sometimes scholars confuse their small truths with the whole truth – and not only scholars do that. It's a common human failing.

I've spared myself a fifth interpretation so as to be able to tell you something of what binds many theologians together today. Scholars do not only argue. They also have shared concerns. This fifth interpretation supplements the others. Its starting point is that in our text Jesus says 'The kingdom of God is in your midst' to the

Pharisees. It has long been thought that this must be a mistake. The evangelist meant the disciples: the kingdom of God is in their midst. He was expressing himself clumsily. But there can be no doubt that the text does mean the Pharisees. They are thought of more positively here than elsewhere in the Gospels. As far as we know, the Pharisees are those who after the destruction of the temple in AD 70 shaped the Judaism that we encounter today. To these forerunners of present-day Judaism Jesus says, 'The kingly rule of God is in your midst.' That puts all interpretations in a new light.

The kingly rule of God will come in the future. Indeed, I said earlier that it was the Jews who asked most intensively about the future kingdom of God. With his preaching of the kingdom of God Jesus belongs fully with his people.

The kingdom of God is in your community. We now also read that differently. Already in the people of Israel we recognize the new community that God wants, a community in which the weak are helped.

Above all we read the fourth interpretation again in a new way: the kingdom of God is in your midst in the person of Jesus. Indeed Jesus belongs in the Jewish people. He and his disciples were Jews.

What does it mean for us that nowadays we are again recognizing the Jewish roots of our faith? Among the German churches the church of Baden has gone further here than many others. And among the theological faculties in Germany the Heidelberg faculty is more open on this point than others. But once again, what does it mean for us that in understanding the Bible we keep being referred back to Judaism? Something very simple, I think. It means that we are becoming ready to learn from Jews about God, even about our question, 'Where is God?'

If a small child were to ask me today, 'Where is God?', I would reply with two Jewish anecdotes. Here's the first:

When Rabbi Yitzhak Meir was a small boy, his mother once took him to a famous teacher. Someone said to him, 'Yitzhak Meir, I will give you a florin if you tell me where God lives.' He replied, 'And I will give you two florins if you tell me where God doesn't live.'

And the second:

A famous rabbi once surprised some learned men who were his guests by asking, 'Where does God live?' They laughed at him. 'What are you saying? Surely the world is full of his glory!' But he answered his own question. 'God lives where people admit him.'

Both anecdotes contain a truth: God is everywhere. But we will only experience him where we admit him: admit him into our history, our community, our hearts. If we recognize that God is where we admit him, then our question changes. In that case we no longer ask 'Where is God? Where can God be experienced? Where do we encounter him?' But we notice that we are being asked, 'Where are you? Where do you admit God into your life? Where are you, Adam? Where are you, Eve? Where do you make room for God?'

Jews encounter this question in their long history with God. Christians encounter it in Jesus. He is the place where God calls on us to be admitted. And then when we admit him into our lives, these small, vanishing, questionable lives take on infinite value. Then in bright days and in dark, in the cosmos and in history, in life and death, we experience the peace of God which passes all our understanding. May this peace of God keep your hearts and minds in Christ Jesus. Amen.

Human Beings as God's Capital
Or, The remarkable story of Pope Callistus

—

(Luke 19.11-27)

While they were listening to this, he went on to tell them a parable, because he was near Jerusalem and the people thought that the kingdom of God was going to appear at once. He said: 'A man of noble birth went to a distant country to have himself anointed king and then to return. So he called ten of his servants and gave them ten pounds. "Put this money to work," he said, "until I come back." But his subjects hated him and sent a delegation after him to say, "We don't want this man to be our king." He was made king, however, and returned home. Then he sent for the servants to whom he had given the money, in order to find out what they had gained with it. The first one came and said, "Sir, your pound has earned ten more." "Well done, my good servant!" his master replied, "Because you have been trustworthy in a very small matter, take charge of ten cities." The second came and said, "Sir, your pound has earned five more." His master answered, "You take charge of five cities." Then another servant came and said, "Sir, here is your pound: I have kept it laid away in a piece of cloth. I was afraid of you, because you are a hard man. You take out what you did not put in and reap what you did not sow." His master replied, "I will judge you by your own words, you wicked servant. You knew, did you, that I am a hard man, taking out what I did not put in, and reaping what I did not sow? Why then didn't you put my money on deposit, so that when I came back, I could have collected it with interest?" Then he said to those standing by, "Take his pound away from him and give it to the one who has ten pounds." "Sir," they said, "He already has ten!" He replied, "I tell you that to everyone who has, more will be given, but as for the one who has nothing, even what he has will be taken away. But those enemies of mine who did not want me to be a king over them – bring them here and kill them in front of me." '

The parable of the talents (or the pounds) makes such demands on preachers that they may well despair of their talent as preachers. This parable is meant to open our eyes to the fact each of us has a gift which only we can develop, resources on which only we can earn interest, a task which only we can perform, competences which only we can make use of. And at the same time it says that only those people are lost who fundamentally rebel against the task posed them by life, a task which no one has given themselves, a task which God gives us. This message has to overcome a great many barriers in us. Here are just four of them.

There is the barrier of feelings of inferiority. Each of us knows moments of depression when we say, 'I can't do anything. All that I've done is worthless and false. Others achieve things so effortlessly, but not me.' No one is free of such despondency, but with some people it intensifies into permanent self-deprecation which no arguments, no recognition, no encouragement seem to be able to break through.

The second barrier is that of convenience. We know that we have some gifts. But we're afraid of allowing them to be drawn out. Moreover we suspect that if we showed too much talent we would be burdened with new tasks. To those who already have tasks, more tasks will be given. Those who succeed in burying their talents, indeed in appearing as idiots, will also be relieved even of the talents that they do have. So it's best to bury not only one's talent but also oneself in the inaccessible niches of life.

The third barrier is that of hurt feelings. We say to ourselves, 'What a gifted person I am, but unfortunately no one takes any notice of me. No one appreciates my qualities, my ideas. Others get all the applause though they're much less able.' It often seems to me that a favourite occupation of German scholars – and those who want to become scholars – is to suffer silently and gently in this way.

Finally there is the fourth barrier, the barrier of obstacles. 'Really,' people tell themselves, 'there's so much I could become. But everything keeps going wrong.' You may be burdened from birth with a body which often fails or isn't very attractive. You had parents who didn't or couldn't show much love and understanding (and that can be really bad). You chose the wrong profession – and to cap it all a partner who did not allow you to develop.

Here the parable says: 'Much is invested in you. You, you yourselves, are God's capital and have to make a profit. You have the opportunity and the duty to make it fruitful – to realize and develop your gifts and indeed yourselves.'

But doesn't the parable make things too simple, even in the face of the harsh realities of life in antiquity? So I would like to tell a story to counterbalance it, one which really happened. It is set at the end of the second and beginning of the third centuries of our era. It's the story of someone who was entrusted with money on which he was to earn interest. This historical biography has two parts. To end with I shall add a third part, a fictitious continuation.

The first part is a career in decline.

This life had already begun at a very lowly level. He had been born as a slave. Even worse, he became the slave of another slave, a member of the imperial household. Certainly he had a very beautiful name. He was called Callistus, 'the most beautiful', and he was a Christian. His master was also a Christian. But none of that helped him very much. It might have been better to call him 'the unlucky one'. After the custom of the time his master put some money at his disposal for setting up a small banking business in Rome. At first things went well. The other Christians in the Roman church supported him and made him loans of all sizes, with which he was to trade. But he had bad luck. He made losses. The losses were so great that he didn't dare look his master in the face. He fled to the port and boarded a ship to escape: a fugitive slave, a desperate man. But his master heard about it and rushed to the port. When Callistus saw him coming, he jumped into the water to kill himself. But even there he had bad luck. Some sailors fished him out and brought him to the bank with loud shouts. His master put him on the treadmill, a punishment for slaves: the Christian master punishing his Christian slave. A number of the other members of the church didn't think that a good thing. They began to plead for Callistus – of course also in the hope that if he were in business again he might still be able to get back some of the money entrusted to him.

But catastrophe struck once more. Callistus went back into business and did his best. But in his attempt to call in arrears he caused offence. The debtors denounced him as a Christian to the city prefect in Rome. There was a trial. Callistus was tortured and flogged, and because he was a Christian was condemned to work in the mines in Sardinia – which meant a drastically shortened life.

I would very much like to know how the unfortunate Callistus understood the parable of the talents. Mustn't he have hated it? Even if he was aware that it was a parable and not about banking - mustn't he have taken offence at its central statement? In the parable, the failure of the lazy slave is attributed to a lack of trust, to mistrust of God and life. This slave says, 'Master, I was afraid of you, because you are a hard man. You take out what you did not put in and reap what you did not sow.' This mistrust *a priori* guides his actions. And it is fully confirmed, indeed more than confirmed. The master indeed proves harsh and unyielding. He even has the one pound that the last slave has taken away from him. This mistrust acts as a self-fulfilling prophecy.

That's the real problem. We do indeed often find God and life just what we expect them to be. If we're full of mistrust, we find only confirmation of our mistrust, indeed we unconsciously arrange our life in such a way that our mistrust is inevitably always confirmed. Everything else gets reinterpreted.

Take the mistrustful student who had the obsession that his professors wanted to kill him. His fellow students spoke kindly to him and said, 'Professors are quite ordinary people, no better than others, but no worse either.' The student wouldn't be convinced. They introduced him to a particularly friendly professor. But the poor student simply said, 'This professor's particularly cunning. To begin with he's disarming me with his kindness, to make it all the easier to kill me later.' We often react to God and life in an equally deluded way. Once someone is seized with a deep mistrust, he or she can reinterpret everything as confirmation of it. Everyday wisdom is also familiar with this in less dramatic contexts. Wilhelm Busch pointed out that those who are suspicious even see sauerkraut as caterpillars. The question is, though, 'Is it enough simply to overcome suspicion?' We could hardly put caterpillars in front of a very trusting person and convince him that this was marvellous sauerkraut and tasted wonderful. No, caterpillars are caterpillars. The evils of life are evils. Blows of fate are blows of fate. Damage is damage. Callistus' condemnation to the mines cannot be reinterpreted. On what pound could he have earned interest there?

Let's now listen to the second part of Callistus' career, a rising career. Commodus, the emperor at that time, had a Christian consort, Marcia, who wanted to do good works. At her instigation all the condemned Christians in Sardinia were freed – including Callistus, who because of this liberation was no longer a slave. Now he was a confessor. So the Roman church gave him a pension and later even appointed him curator of the catacombs. At that time the Roman church was beginning to bury all believers in its own cemeteries. Possibly this was the work of Callistus. A catacomb bears his name. Among those buried there we find typical slaves' names. Callistus looked after the poor and the slaves. In doing this he must have gained so much trust that he was even elected bishop of Rome – over the head of a much more aristocratic rival.

This man took his revenge by writing a bad obituary – long after the death of Callistus (it took historical-critical scholarship to put it right). What did he accuse Callistus of?

His first charge was that Callistus had allowed women of high social status to live with slaves and freemen outside marriage. These women would have lost their privileges if they had become formally married to slaves. Callistus gave church recognition to these 'wild marriages', which were not particularly 'wild'. He prized happiness and loyalty to the other partner above the official law. He is said even to have allowed priests to remarry. And of course his opponents insinuated that he wanted to allow 'sinful lusts' to have free rein. An amazing bishop! One might sigh and say that bishops of Rome nowadays are no longer what they were.

The second charge was that Callistus made it easy for sinners to return into the church. His favourite parable is said to have been the parable of the tares in the wheat. The wheat is the sinners, and they have to be tolerated patiently in the church.

The third charge was that Callistus was a heretic. He was against all attempts to subordinate Jesus to the Father or to separate him from the Father. Here his most important motive was the idea that the Father suffered with the Son, that he was not exempt from suffering, and that the Father identified with the scourged Jesus as he did with him, the scourged and maltreated Callistus.

It's not difficult to combine these three charges. Callistus was a Christian who had himself suffered social discrimination, who knew the charge that he was a sinner and a failure, and who had suffered. This Callistus had come to grief doing business on borrowed money. But precisely for that reason he had another kind of capital which he could increase to the benefit of his church: the treasure of the experience of his suffering. He could understand slaves who entered into 'wild marriages' with well-to-do ladies. He could understand failures who were despised. He could understand the poor people for whom he built and looked after his catacombs.

We too should think like that. We shouldn't just stare at the many internal and external obstacles to the development of our gifts. Even the painful things in our lives can become a blessing for us and for others. How could we understand those who despair of ever being worth everything had we ourselves not been through the dark tunnel of a depression? How could we understand the hidden anxieties of those who take it easy had we ourselves not been bogged down in inertia? How can we cope with those who feel sorry for themselves if we haven't experienced in ourselves how paralysing it can be not to be appreciated? How can we accept the handicapped and the incapacitated unreservedly if we have not been rubbed raw – often with very small hurts – and learned how difficult it is to cope with them?

Those who have many gifts should be grateful. But those who sense a lack of gifts are called to by God through the Bible. Blessed are you poor, you sorrowful, you hungry and thirsty. For it is out of people like you that God builds his kingdom, out of people who often limp and hobble inwardly and outwardly, out of the weary and the heavy-laden, the weak and the sick. A gift is entrusted to all of you. And we can learn all this from the story of Callistus, for he too was 'weary and heavy laden'.

To end with, I would like to add a fictitious continuation to his career, a continuation in our time. Imagine that Callistus had to defend himself before a synod today over his decision to give theological recognition to relationships outside marriage. Of course he wouldn't be accused, as he was then, of wanting to encourage 'sinful lusts'. Things are put differently these days. It would be said that he was leading people astray, into the hedonism of modern fulfilment and self-development, so that they put personal happiness above responsibility and duty. I imagine that he would make the following defence, beginning like this:

'Dear brothers and sisters,

You make it too simple when you refer to the Christian faith in criticizing those who take the path to self-fulfilment. We all have the task of looking for this path and taking it. All of us, men and women. We all have the duty of increasing and developing what the Creator has invested in us and entrusted to us. We are God's capital. And that should produce interest. Anyone who thinks that God is against such fulfilment is imagining an envious God, as though God grudged his creatures growth and development. However, I would like to make two things clear to our modern fellow men and women, against the background of my own experience.

Fulfilment is not to be had without suffering. Indeed the suffering on the way to fulfilment is often particularly acute, because here we come to grief not only on external circumstances but also on ourselves, on our careers, on what we have undertaken. Here we are deeply vulnerable. So if we see anyone in difficulties on the path to fulfilment, we shouldn't say, "You were on the wrong road." Let's try to teach such people that one can grow through pain. That even in our relations with one another we can grow through suffering at the hands of others. That personal growth takes place through crises, through a "Die and become" which Christians associate with the death and resurrection of Jesus.

And a second insight is important to me. Nowadays we often encounter a kind of metaphysics of the market economy among people on the path to fulfilment: the trust that the capital invested in us must simply be developed without hindrance and that an invisible hand will direct all things for the good. If both partners develop with all their being, that can only bring them together. There is no tension between fulfilment and altruism, though experience tells against this. Particularly in partnership, isn't there a good deal of fulfilment at the other's expense? Here, too, we shouldn't say, "So either one or both must renounce fulfilment." No, we must make it clear that according to Christian faith there can be reconciliation between fulfilment and altruism – precisely when we experience others as part of ourselves. When the other is as near to us as a member of the same body. When the suffering of others is our suffering, their joy is our joy; but also, conversely, when our joys are their joys and our pain is their pain. That is precisely what Paul says about those who are bound together through the Spirit in Christ.'

By now the synod has become restless. It is not only that Callistus has been talking too long. He is getting off the subject. 'What has this to do with the problem of free partnerships?' someone asks.

Callistus replies, 'A great deal! For the image for this deep bond in the New Testament is marriage. If two people are so closely bound together that they can understand even suffering at the hands of the other as a growth in their partnership, if the other's joy is their own joy and even the other's fulfilment has become part of their own – then the two of them have become one body and one flesh. In that case they are a marriage. And I am prepared to recognize them as a marriage before the highest of all authorities, even if they hesitate to seek recognition from lesser authorities. There are very different reasons for this hesitation. Against the background of my own experience not all of them are clear to me, but some are: some old women are afraid of losing claims to pensions (perhaps through the sudden death of their elderly partner). Some young women are afraid that if they are married they won't be able to develop their talents in their profession any more. Especially in Christian circles, the very fact of being married is often regarded as a moral argument against looking for a job. Married women would find it too much and would be depriving others of the chance to work. Moreover, this is seen as just a selfish urge for fulfilment. Others may differ from me here. At any rate' – Callistus says – 'at that time they decided in Rome that women shouldn't suffer any social disadvantage as a result of their partnerships and marriages. Certainly the problems are rather different now – and much more complex. Certainly I made my decision at a time when the bishops of Rome were not as infallible as they are today. But precisely that makes my decision worth thinking about.

So please don't pass too hasty judgment on women who think that they can't develop their talents in traditional marriage. God's capital comes up against many obstacles to growth in this world. They're not only to be found within men and women, but can also lie in external circumstances. So we shouldn't be content with urging individuals to earn interest on their pounds. We must also fight for conditions in which that is more possible. For with every human being an irreplaceable spark of light has come into the world. And it is also up to us that it isn't quenched, but that the light increases and makes this world its home. All of us can contribute to that. We all have that as our task. We have all been given a pound for that, on which we can earn interest.'

And because Callistus knows that many have people have a different view about marriage – and because I, too, know that many people will not be able to agree with me, I would prefer to end with the words, 'And may the peace of God which passes all our understanding keep your hearts in Jesus Christ. Amen.'

Doubting Thomas
And the credibility of the Easter message

—

(John 20.19-29)

On the evening of that first day of the week, when the disciples were together with the doors locked for fear of the Jews, Jesus came and stood among them and said, 'Peace be with you!' After he said this, he showed them his hands and side. The disciples were overjoyed when they saw the Lord. Again Jesus said, 'Peace be with you! As the Father has sent me, I am sending you.' And with that he breathed on them and said, 'Receive the Holy Spirit. If you forgive anyone his sins, they are forgiven. If you do not forgive them they are not forgiven.' Now Thomas (called Didymus), one of the Twelve, was not with the disciples when Jesus came. So the other disciples told him, 'We have seen the Lord!' But he said to them, 'Unless I see the nail marks in his hands and put my finger where the nails were, and put my hand into his side, I will not believe it.' A week later his disciples were in the house again, and Thomas was with them. Though the doors were locked, Jesus came and stood among them and said, 'Peace be with you!' Then he said to Thomas, 'Put your finger here; see my hands. Reach out your hand and put it into my side. Stop doubting and believe.' Thomas said to him. 'My Lord and my God!' Then Jesus told him, 'Because you have seen me, you have believed; blessed are those who have not seen and yet have believed.'

Doubting Thomas is often more alive in us than the risen Jesus. For we are all doubters, though to differing degrees. All believers are also doubters. There are people with a faith which consists more in doubt as to whether the widespread repudiation of faith is right. They are beginners in doubt. Then there are more advanced doubters. They doubt everything, one thing after another, but for them the question how much Christian faith they still retain has become more interesting. And then there are mature doubters.

117

They have few certainties, but these give them enough support to leave many questions open. For some, the Easter message also belongs among these open questions. Indisputably, like Thomas, we can follow Jesus, be seized by his Spirit, and stand perplexed before the Easter stories. So today I would like to join a modern Thomas in different lessons in doubt.

The first lesson begins when our Thomas decides to study theology. He tells himself that it is important to get to the bottom of things. That means study: in Greek, with a concordance, lexicon, grammar, commentary. The result can be summed up briefly: the evidence for the Easter stories is not all that bad. The best known individual witnesses have a special relationship with Jesus: Peter denied Jesus, Paul persecuted his followers, James was his brother. Women are also mentioned; at that time their evidence didn't count for much and so is all the weightier today. The traditions are also old. Paul says that he received them from others and handed them on while many eye-witnesses were still alive. The scholars let a good deal of dust settle on the empty tomb. Some say one thing, some another, and most nothing at all. In the meantime our modern Thomas has read 103 books on the subject, but as an experienced doubter he tells himself, 'Perhaps there will be a really convincing argument in the 104th book,' and so on. When he gets to the 120th he thinks of that unknown book which a still unknown lecturer will write in 150 years and which he will never ever be able to read – the book which perhaps will finally bring the truth to light. Thomas is very doubtful about that. For he will never know what will be known after his death. And worse, even if he did know it, he would still be in the world of ideas, arguments and hypotheses. He will never be able to get out of this world in order to compare reality with it. We all sit in it, like the spider in her web. And he asks himself, 'How do we distinguish at all between fantasy and reality, imagination and what actually is?'

As he has no time to read another 120 books on this question, he appeals to his everyday experience. We notice reality by the fact that it is painful. The person who is wounded in the side has no philosophical problems in demonstrating the reality of the outside world at that particular moment. When something disruptive and devastating – like sickness or injustice – enters our lives, we are convinced that we are up against something real. Thomas is aware that he is looking for the pain which makes reality known. Marks of wounds are not only the signs by which the Lord is recognized, but also reality itself. The world of books, in which he met only a dull trace of human pain, has failed him there. There he lives in the world of assumptions and ideas, but not in the world where people suffer, where they are tortured and crucified. However, Thomas also recognizes that in the world of books there is an analogy to the painful encounter with reality. There, too, we feel most intensively that we are struggling not only with our own ideas, but with reality, when we have to correct an assumption, when we have to subject a theory to the pressure of the facts. That also hurts. That's painful. Here Thomas has learned the first lesson in doubt, the historical-critical lesson. He has arrived at the insight that he has to go out into life, which can be very painful.

Some fellow students understand his problem and introduce him to a group in which people laugh at his historical-critical phase. Their association calls itself 'Soul and Symbol'. Their central doctrine is that what the Bible says is part of a general symbolic human language which discloses unconscious depths in us. Authentic reality lies there. The initiate, who on the way to the shaman is swallowed up by a monster in order to appropriate its powers, has the same experiences as Jonah, who is swallowed up by the whale and spat out to new life. The experience of Jonah repeats itself in the death and resurrection of Jesus, and in all Christians who allow themselves to be crucified and buried with him in order to begin a new life. All these images and symbols embody the same universal truth: we become ourselves only when we detach ourselves from our old life, with its pain and fear of death. But the new life announces itself in a dream. In the dream God speaks to human beings with the help of the universal symbolic language. And because historical-critical scholars do not know this language, they remain on the surface of things.

To begin with, doubting Thomas was fascinated: if the death and resurrection of Jesus are images of processes in us – images of a radical change of life which takes place in the unconscious and is removed from conscious direction – then we can experience its truth directly. We feel it in ourselves. We have certainty. For this truth is part of ourselves.

Doubting Thomas had only one problem that his symbol friends couldn't solve. He didn't dream such nice dreams as people expected in those circles. His dreams were confused, chopped up, often bloodthirsty, usually obscene, and frequently full of anxiety about death. For a long time he had echoes of childhood memories of night-time air raids. Only rarely did he have a dream which seemed to him to be a revelation. One such dream went like this.

He had to go through a long, dark tunnel. And he immediately felt that this was death. Through the tunnel he saw death coming to meet him. It was a great insect with a giant sting, the sting of death, which would pierce him. He had a terrible anxiety, but could not run away. Then he suddenly noticed the monster becoming uncertain. The anxiety in him appeared to communicate itself to the monster. It moved anxiously aside, as though he were surrounded by an invisible protective wall. And he became increasingly bold, as though he were immune against the sting of death. He passed the monster, and saw a light getting brighter, a long way down the dark tunnel. He woke up. It was light. The remarkable thing was that the next night he again dreamed a dream which seemed to be a correction of the first dream. A doctor told him that he was terminally ill; the stone of the anguish of death lay heavy on his heart, and he could not move it away.

So Thomas learned that the pains which torment us even in our dreams are not just pains of self-realization. Death and finitude are harsh external factors – not just inner processes. Certainly the Easter message must speak a language of symbols which penetrates deep within us. But it must itself come from outside – just as death and finitude come to us from outside. So Thomas again went in search of reality, of an external reality. He sought not only the pains of his own self-realization but the pain which reveals absolute reality, the 'wounds of the Lord'.

In the third stage of his doubt he got into a circle of esoteric friends who promised him contact with a reality outside human experience. They told him of thought-transference, telepathy, second sight, and prognostic intimations, and stressed that this was only the beginning. Thomas listened to them avidly. It was the most normal thing imaginable for dead people to make themselves known to their relatives who were still alive. Here Thomas, with his doubts, seemed a heretic, an outsider. Much of what he was told sounded completely credible. He didn't want to exclude the possibility that there is a transfer of information from the dying (and the dead) to those close to them, in a way which we cannot perceive. But when he was invited to take part in a seance in which they wanted to make such a spirit appear he refused in some perturbation: there was a big difference between a 'sign' which appeared spontaneously and such human manipulation of the abnormal. Hastily and in confusion he left the circle of esoterics.

Fortunately he had an African friend. This friend told him that at home, people thought it quite natural to be in contact with the dead. In their church they had other difficulties with the Easter message from people in Europe. Here in Europe people asked, 'How can a dead person be recreated from nothingness?' But at home people asked, 'What's special about that? Is Jesus alive in a different way from our ancestors, who appear to us in dreams and give helpful advice?' Here the story of doubting Thomas was a real help. Thomas didn't want just to see the risen Jesus but to feel his wounds, the signs of execution and torture. He wanted to assure himself that something is stronger than the violent death which put an end to Jesus. Many black people in his homeland suffered violent death; the situation was particularly desperate in the south. Here they faced a perfect system of oppression in comparison with which the experiences of the ancestors paled into insignifance. The ancestors simply had not reckoned on so much wickedness. But in the Christians who encountered injustice there, who were arrested and tortured, the power of the resurrection encountered the hope of triumph over violence. Christians in Europe should learn from these people to see in the wounds of Jesus the traces of suffering and oppression.

The conversation with this African sorted out a good deal. But it raised new questions: Thomas would never be able to share the natural way in which other cultures accepted contact with the beyond. He was not an African. He lived in a culture of doubt and scepticism. And he was proud to do so. If the Easter message was to affect him, it had to speak at the centre of this culture of doubt and from there penetrate the depths of the soul and the limits of experience. Thomas had to undergo a last lesson in doubt.

So he joined a club of radical freethinkers. Here the theory was that anyone who is looking for meaning has gone wrong and is a victim of faulty psychological development or a physical malfunction. Human life is a tiny peripheral phenomemon on a small planet. The more clearly human beings see their position in the gigantic universe, the more painfully they become aware of the meaninglessness of existence: a fortuitous phenomenon in which matter has organized itself in an over-complicated way so that sometimes it reflects about itself too much. Human organisms are programmed for self-preservation and therefore they contain programmes for values and criteria. These are necessary for the functioning of society and the psychological balance of the individual, but otherwise are an illusion which suggests that all labour will one day be worth while, whereas everything is inexorably moving towards a cosmic death in heat or cold. The wise person sees through this illusion. He, Thomas, is also invited to join the privileged circle of those wise people who have no illusions. Granted, the loss of all illusions is painful to begin with. But one gets something incomparably better in return: a view of reality as it really is, beyond our wishes and dreams. With this message they left him.

Thomas asked himself, 'Was that the pain which was to make him feel ultimate reality? Did it consist in the crucifixion of all illusions, so that the naked truth could arise from their failure? Was the world-process a giant stream falling into the abyss – which people swim on and know nothing about? Does a benevolent total illusion protect them from looking into nothingness?' Only a few learned people know this. But they pass their insight on in whispers. For they have nothing to offer to make their nihilism humanly tolerable – apart from the privileged pleasure of being learned and seeing through everything.

Here I interrupt the story of Thomas to insert myself into his inner dialogue. I think that what the radical freethinkers say is an authentic possibility for experiencing and interpreting the world. It is far too familiar to me personally for me to be able to interpret it away. It is 'nihilism' – the discovery that nothing in the world as it is experienced can provide unconditional support in life and death. Certainly I find much occasion in this world for a limited trust – a trust which is conditional upon my body functioning, upon society keeping on the rails, and our having some happiness. Thank God we all grow up with such a conditional natural trust! But when confronted with reality, this courage to live is crucified. It dies many deaths – through experiences of the unavoidable defeats in life, but also through insights into what is. However, a miracle keeps happening. This courage to life arises anew out of nothing. In the end I can no more justify and explain it than why the world exists at all. Indeed this new unconditional courage to live is itself a creation out of nothing. Nowhere do I feel more clearly than in this courage to live, the power that calls nothing into being, that gives life to the dead, that brings about and sustains existence at every moment. In it I experience God's creative power. Without nihilism I would never understand what *creatio ex nihilo* means – creation out of nothing.

The Easter message tells all of us that this power which creates out of nothing has entered our lives. It is stronger than the nothingness into which the stream of reality disappears. It is the same power from which this stream comes. The Easter message does not primarily seek to disclose some esoteric back room of the world or the unconscious cellar of the heart – though there is no doubt that it does all that, that it can do all that – but it confronts us above all with what creates and sustains all reality, from the remotest galaxies to the tiniest slipper animalcule, from the rhythms of life to our breathing, thought and being.

This power calls out to you: 'Those who hear my voice have already passed from death to life. They are given new courage to live, courage which is created out of nothing.'

It calls out, 'Bring love into this world. For only by love can you recognize that you have passed from death to life. Those who do not love remain in death.' That is what the first letter of John says.

It breathes its spirit into you, just as it breathed its spirit into the lifeless Adam, and gives you the task of forgiving guilt, healing the sick, making the sorrowful glad. It keeps removing the stone of anxiety about death from your hearts and robs death of its sting. It does not leave you in the tunnels of terror, and in the dark valley it is with you.

This power can be recognized by the marks of its wounds. It encounters you in the sorrows of life, where despair and nihilism are abroad.

This power is addressed by the Thomas who has come to believe when he says to Jesus, 'My Lord and my God', and calls Jesus God, as he is so called only at the beginning of the Gospel of John. For this power surrounds us always and everywhere. Or, as the Gospel of John puts it, 'All things were made by it and without it was not anything made that was made. It is the light for human beings, and in its light we see light.'

Let me end with a very imperfect image of the way in which I imagine the presence of this power. It seems to me like a giant field of electromagnetic waves for which we have no natural organs, but which we detect by its effects, say when we represent its structure with iron filings or demonstrate its power with sparks. It is present everywhere. Only sometimes a spark strikes our limited everyday world. The Easter experiences are such a spark. It is not the appearances that are important, but the field of force from which they come and which surrounds us everywhere. We can always trace this field of force, even when the Easter appearances fade into the past. None of us could be witness to them. But the spark of an unconditional courage to live and die can fly into each of us. And then each of us may relate to himself or herself the beatitude, 'Blessed are those who have not seen and yet have believed.'

And may the peace of God which passes all our understanding keep our hearts and minds in Jesus Christ our Lord, Amen.

The Restlessness of the Spirit
A sermon for Pentecost

(Acts 2.1-13)

When the day of Pentecost came, they were all together in one place. Suddenly a sound like the blowing of a violent wind came from heaven and filled the whole house where they were sitting. They saw what seemed to be tongues of fire that separated and came to rest on each of them. All of them were filled with the Holy Spirit and began to speak in other tongues as the Spirit enabled them. Now there were staying in Jerusalem devout Jews from every nation under heaven. When they heard this sound, a crowd came together in bewilderment, because each one heard them speaking in his own language. Utterly amazed, they asked: 'Are not all these men who are speaking Galileans? Then how is it that each of us hears them in his own native language? Parthians, Medes and Elamites; residents of Mesopotamia, Judea and Cappadocia, Pontus and Asia, Phrygia and Pamphylia, Egypt and the parts of Libya near Cyrene; visitors from Rome (both Jews and converts to Judaism), Cretans and Arabs – we hear them declaring the wonders of God in our own tongues.' Amazed and perplexed, they asked one another, 'What does this mean?' Some, however, made fun of them and said, 'They have had too much wine.'

Pentecost is the feast of the Spirit, a feast which has particular significance in a university city. Precisely where the human spirit develops – often with remarkable interference – it is important to reflect on another spirit, a strange spirit, the Spirit of God.

That is a spirit which has esoteric and enigmatic characteristics: a fire which does not destroy, a storm which does not devastate. Its appearance is depicted as the appearance of God: with rushing wind and fire and the opening of heaven. It is as omnipresent as wind and air, and yet enters into people, changes them, becomes the subject of their speech and action. This Spirit is an alien spirit, but a spirit

125

which overcomes alienation. It overcomes the alienation between God and human beings: it creates communication where there was no communication. For this it chooses a strange form of linguistic behaviour – speaking with tongues. But precisely in this unusual way it overcomes linguistic barriers. And it founds a community in which each may be confident of the help of others. That is what I want to reflect on now: on the twofold alienation which is overcome by the Spirit.

Let's begin with alienation between human beings. If you had asked a Christian in the first century what attracted him to the community, he would have answered, 'Because the Spirit is there!' And if you had pressed him to be more precise, he would have answered, 'There are people among us from all over the world, Jews, Parthians, Medes, Cappadocians, people from Pontus, Asia Minor and Phrygia – but in the community we all belong together.' He could have quoted from the letters of Paul: 'For we were all baptized by one Spirit into one body – whether Jews or Greeks, slave or free – and we were all given the one Spirit to drink' (I Cor.12.13). Precisely that was what made the earliest Christian communities attractive: people came closer to one another than anywhere else in society. The experience of the Spirit meant getting closer, breaking down the social gulf between poor and rich, between Jews and Gentiles, between masters and slaves. The experience of the Spirit meant the overcoming of loneliness – which could also be experienced at that time, as the moving laments of Gnostic groups show.

But why is our Spirit, our capacity for empathy, not enough? Why don't we build the bridges to other people by our own powers?

We do a good deal here. But there are limits. We are all imprisoned in our 'spirits' as we are in our own skins. All that is, exists for us only as long as we exist. Each of us is a world history. A world history is buried under each tombstone. What do we know of all these world histories before and alongside us? Every day they cross our own histories. Every day there are little world wars and cosmic catastrophes.

Let me give an example to make this clearer. Imagine two colleagues. Both are working in an office. Mr A needs a stapler with a long arm for his papers. He knows that Mr X has such a stapler.

He's about to get up to borrow it. Then he imagines Mr X. He sees his face, his smile. No, not his smile, his smirk. Didn't Mr X smirk in a remarkable way the last time he was with him? Now it occurs to Mr A that the smirk was no coincidence. Recently Mr X had torpedoed his suggestions at a meeting. And afterwards he had been standing with other people. Of course, he had been gossiping about him. Now scales seem to fall from Mr A's eyes. Everything is clear. Mr X is systematically trying to disparage him. He can't let that happen. No, now he must go and tell Mr X what he thinks of him. The scoundrel! Mr A rushes into the other room and shouts at the amazed Mr X, 'Keep your damned stapler! To hell with it! And I've had enough of your damned smirk.'

Such episodes occur every day. People get caught up in their own destructive fantasies, and lose contact with the real Mr X. They fight with a shadow of their own spirit. This is being shut in on oneself, imprisonment in one's own world.

What leads to bizarre conflicts in individual life is normal in the relationship between nations and societies: nations constantly get entangled in a destructive dialogue with themselves about the others. But then it is not about the other's smirk, but about its rockets, economic power or ideology. Here our reason often proves to be only a weak corrective: often we seem to find the most reasonable arguments possible specially in order to attribute the worst intentions to others.

That, then, is our situation. We are shut in on ourselves – individually and collectively. And that is a curse, a danger – a fatal danger.

In a Pentecost sermon the obvious thing now would be to depict the Holy Spirit as the power which overcomes such imprisonment. That is not untrue. Before that, however, it is necessary to make something else clear: not only being shut in on oneself, but also feelings of empathy can become a curse, a torment and a burden.

What do I mean by that? Let's take another image: the many radio waves which are whirling round this room at any time. If we installed a receiver we could make them audible. Then we would find that the whole room is constantly full of information, words and sounds, without our being aware of the fact. It's the same with signals between human beings. The whole everyday world is full of them. Once we become aware of them and install a receiver, we become confused, even after listening for only a short time: from all sides cries for help which we have not heard before keep coming to us. Once one becomes sensitive to them, even small gestures can be decoded as a concealed cry: a stiff handshake, a break in the voice, a confused sideways glance. Think of all that is unsaid between the words! Once we have deciphered the code and opened ourselves up to other people – once we have lost that self-interested egocentricity which decides what to receive and what not – we will soon long for the time when we were balanced egocentrics.

But the Pentecost story speaks not only of overcoming individual barriers, but of overcoming barriers between the nations. The Spirit brings about communication between the nations. Here too we have to ask: isn't such communication often a burden? Don't you often find a picture of a hungry child coming to you from the Third World and catching your imagination? This hungry child with the disillusioned eyes has the same right to live as you do. It's only chance that you're not in its place. It's just one child among many suffering children. It's just one of those who labour and are heavy laden on this earth. If we could make their cries for help audible – as we could make the hidden radio waves audible – this church would be full of an uncanny roaring. The voices of the oppressed, the maimed, the tortured and the sick, the abandoned and the dying, would unite in this roar: the whole sighing of creation would become a mighty storm. It would go through us like fire. We couldn't bear it. It would be too much. It would destroy us.

Again it emerges that being shut in on oneself is a curse, but being open to others just as quickly becomes an intolerable burden.

Now we're at the point where we have to speak of that other alienation which is addressed in the Pentecost story – the alienation between God and human beings. If we have complete empathy with someone else, so that we lose our own centre, if we make the other's problems our problems and are driven by them to the point of being possessed, we have failed to take note of the distance between God and human beings – we are human beings, not God. Our horizon of experience, our capacity for empathy, our capacities for helping are always limited. Those who cross this frontier inwardly will fantasize themselves into the role of being responsible for everything, of attempting to play God. Such people overestimate their power to a dangerous degree. Such people deny their own finitude.

Our spirit is too limited to bind us to all human beings. But we can bind ourselves to God's Spirit and God's Spirit can bind itself to us. God can do what we cannot. God can be present in each individual. God can suffer with each individual. God can rejoice with each individual. God can surmount those frontiers that we cannot.

We would fall apart if we thought that we had to decode and answer all the signals for help that we receive. But if we trust that the Spirit of God hears all these cries for help, indeed that this Spirit sends it on behalf of human beings – then we are bound up with all people. Then we know that the suffering of someone somewhere in Latin America also affects our life. But we also know that such people are not alone: God's Spirit is with them, the same Spirit that also moves and drives our life.

'But,' some people will remark, 'isn't that cold comfort? Doesn't that amount to saying "Let God bother about the others. In that case I don't need to do anything"?' No, it's not cheap comfort. The Spirit of God is familiar with suffering. It is the Spirit of Jesus Christ. It is the Spirit of someone who himself is one of those creatures who have been maltreated. It is the Spirit which expressed for all time an unconditional protest against all suffering, and also did so vicariously for those who cannot protest.

Above all, the spirit which sensitizes us to the suffering and pains of other people is the spirit of those who act against such suffering and pain. It is a spirit of mission and a common task. In the fellowship of this spirit we are not alone. We may trust that it motivates people everywhere – and not just us – to overcome their selfishness and laziness and act on behalf of others. This spirit is experienced in the community of believers. It gives us as Christians a common task in this world which we could not perform alone.

What does this task look like? The Pentecost story gives us clear indications. After the outpouring of the Holy Spirit and Peter's Pentecost sermon it depicts the effects of the Spirit. These consist in more than an emotional overcoming of distance. We also read of a material redistribution of possessions in favour of the needy. Just as the Pentecost story is introduced with the words 'they were all together in one place', so it ends: 'All the believers were together and had everything in common. Selling their possessions and goods, they gave to anyone as he had need' (Acts 2.44f.). The fellowship of the Holy Spirit – that includes readiness to even out possessions, readiness to give away.

A community which binds people together is possible only where this readiness is present. Where this readiness is not present, the Spirit of Jesus is not alive either.

Let's remember that both being shut in ourselves and having a boundless capacity for empathy are torture for us. We waver to and fro between them. The Spirit of God gives a new perspective: it overcomes the distance between God and man and provides the basis for a new relationship between human beings. For when the Spirit of God takes hold of us, then through it we are bound up with all human beings – with all who suffer and all who act against suffering. Then we can open ourselves to other people near and far, without anxiety that it will prove too much for us. Then we have a limited mission. Then we know that we can help, along with others, and even if we achieve only a little, then we can stand an enormous amount. Then – in the fellowship of the Holy Spirit – we can risk losing our life in order to find it. Then we experience that blessing with which I would like to end: 'And may the peace of God which passes all our understanding keep your heads and minds in Jesus Christ. Amen.'

Science as the Art of Gardening
and the absence of the gardener

(Romans 8.15)

Every semester is a new attempt to make progress in the natural and the humane sciences and to win over new generations to scientific thinking. Therefore the first service in the semester always essentially has only one theme: reflecting on scientific activity before God. I didn't seek out our text with a view to this task. Nor was it the intention of its author to say anything about science. But precisely for that reason he can perhaps shed light on our problems from quite a different perspective. The text comes from the letter of Paul to the Romans (8.15).

For you did not receive a spirit that makes you a slave again to fear, but you received the Spirit (which is given at the time) of acceptance in place of the Son. And by him we cry, 'Abba, Father.'

First the translation of the text needs a brief comment. Lexically the translation 'sonship' is correct. But if we translate that way we get tangled up in those problems to which feminist theology has rightly drawn our attention. Sonship is a masculine concept. It can be understood in such a way as to exclude women. So should we say 'childhood'? A little later Paul speaks of 'children of God'. But if we do that we lose something important. The son is contrasted with the servant. In other words, the concept of the 'son' contains the very characteristics of coming of age and autonomy, freedom and independence, which children don't have. So should we speak of sons and daughters, of sonship and daughterhood? But in that case we would be making a distinction which appears nowhere in the text, as though being a 'son' or a 'daughter' of God might possibly be different things. Perhaps we should paraphrase the whole passage: 'You did not receive a spirit of dependence which creates fear, but you have been adopted by God, so that in this Spirit we cry, 'Abba, Father!' But even then questions still remain. Why do we say 'Abba, Father', and not 'Imma, Mother'?

But now to the theme of our service: scientific activity before God – something we are already engaged in. It is highly dubious whether God is very pleased at seeing men and women having such differing roles in scientific activity. God can hardly be pleased that scientific activity is still largely a male concern. There are no scientific arguments for that. Here we find a bit of irrational dependence in the midst of so rational a matter as science. And that has in fact brought us directly to the theme of science and dependence.

The first part of Paul's sentence can be applied directly to science. Let me repeat it again. 'For you did not receive a spirit that makes you a slave again to (or dependent on) fear!' Science seeks to reduce dependence on fear, not least the fear of religious powers. We are all aware that the preaching of sermons in churches does not do away with the need for lightning conductors. Lightning conductors reduce anxiety. Without science there would be no lightning conductors. The so-called humane sciences certainly don't construct lightning conductors – but they too seek to free people from dependence and fear: from dependence on restrictive traditions and prejudices, for example from dependence on patriarchal traditions, by investigating the reasons, function, origin and transformation of all those convictions with which women were discriminated against. We can therefore rephrase Paul's sentence like this: 'You who have received the spirit of science have not received a spirit of dependence which creates fear again.' At least, that is how one could paraphrase the ideal of the scientific spirit. That is how it should be. But it isn't.

In reality isn't the opposite also true: that science causes anxiety – not only anxiety about studies and examinations, but also anxieties which affect everyone? Let me mention three of them.

First, since science governs the whole of our lives, the whole of our lives are involved in a basic human problem about science: by the time we have laboriously acquired some knowledge, it is already out of date. In a world shaped by science there is an invisible label on everything: 'Past scientific "sell by" date'. It may be the way in which we bring up our children, our diet, or how we blow our noses. Probably there is a wise book somewhere which shows that we do everything wrong – including blowing our noses! Science devalues every form of life as we live it. Here we come up against anxiety over human finitude: we don't know everything; perhaps some of our knowledge is wrong. And indeed what we think we know is often wrong.

Secondly, the consequences of science are submerging us. We can't see the consequences of our scientific knowledge and sometimes feel helplessly at the mercy of its own dynamics – most clearly in the development of new military technology. We know that when a perfect defence-system or first-strike capability is available, but for the moment available only to one side, we all need to hold our breath. And here too we come up against a basic human anxiety, which is connected with responsibility for the consequences of our own action. This anxiety can be limited where consequences can be seen and calculated. But precisely that is not the case with the development promoted by science.

And finally a third anxiety: anxiety about power or about the powerful. Science costs a tremendous amount of money. Those who have power and money have incomparably greater opportunities to direct research and technological developments – and they use it for their own ends. Only in a few states in this world is political power under adequate control. What becomes of science in the hands of the powerful? Power always tends to corrupt. And absolute power corrupts absolutely. But science is power, and like all power can corrupt.

Those are three anxieties associated with that science which is meant to free us from anxiety and fear: anxiety about human finitude, anxiety about our responsibility and anxiety about our uncontrollable power.

It would be tempting now to go straight on to the second part of Paul's sentence. It would be tempting to say that in the spirit of sonship, in the spirit of being members of the family of God, human beings can finally bear their finitude, perceive their responsibility and control their excesses of power. All that is true. Even those who are not very used to sermons will know that this will be the answer. But it would be naive to give it at this stage. It would be naive, because science does not promote this 'family' spirit which binds us to God. On the contrary, science is methodologically atheistic. In other words, when it comes to verifying or disproving a scientific hypothesis, the acceptance or rejection of God is not a valid factor. I would like to illustrate the problem with the famous parable of the gardener.

Once upon a time two explorers came upon a clearing in the jungle. In the clearing were growing many flowers and many weeds. One explorer says, 'Some gardener must tend this plot.' The other disagrees. 'There is no gardener.' So they set up a barbed wire fence. They electrify it. They patrol with bloodhounds. But no shrieks ever suggest that some intruder has received a shock. No movements of the wire ever betray an invisible climber. The bloodhounds never give cry. Yet still the believer is not convinced. 'But there is a gardener, invisible, intangible, insensible to electric shocks, a gardener who has no scent and makes no sound, a gardener who comes secretly to look after the garden which he loves.' At last the sceptic despairs, 'But what remains of your original assertion? Just how does what you call an invisible, intangible, eternally elusive gardener differ from an imaginary gardener or even from no gardener at all?'

The parable illustrates better than many abstract words the relationship between faith and science – and that means the situation of believers in science and the university. Let me make three comments on this fine parable.

First, both the believer and the sceptic are irrefutable. However, they are certainly wrong on one point. They think that they are discussing whether one can interpret reality in religious terms or not. But they are both unbelievers. In the middle of the jungle they come upon surprising and improbable order – and how do they react? They debate and experiment. What would a believer do? Wouldn't a believer be amazed at this miraculous order and regard it as a task to maintain it, so that the jungle of life doesn't swallow it up? Wouldn't the believer first of all sense that this garden has to be preserved? It's endangered. And it is our great task to preserve it and develop it. In short, to believers, this garden seems like a task which they have not set themselves, but which they have found, or by which they have been found. And that's not all.

There is a second reaction: for the believer the garden isn't just a task, but is first of all a gift, a present. The spontaneous reaction of the believer will be: we must celebrate having found this garden. We can't simply go past it. After such a discovery you must give praise and thanks. And that amounts to founding a cult, a religion. Alongside, indeed even before, the ethical answer to the existence of the garden there is a liturgical, ritual or cultic one.

Thirdly and lastly, our believer would become poetic. He or she would invent a story and tell of a gardener who once built a garden and put people in it, with the task of looking after it. There is no disputing that there is a good deal of fantasy in this story. It's poetry. Here our sceptic would probably object and say, 'Why this poetry? Doesn't science consist in demystifying the garden and letting such stories die out?' Hardly. The parable of the gardener is itself a poem – and it shows how high the status of poetry is as a form of knowledge. Indeed it suggests more than the author intended. We should consider that for a moment.

Let's look once again at this story of a sceptic. Here we encounter science in a not particularly attractive light: it constructs barbed-wire fences, patrols with bloodhounds and installs electrified barriers. Does the fact that God evades such methods tell against him or against these methods?

Moreover, both these explorers seem like colonizers, like foreign conquerors who invade a virgin continent in which they are not at home, like arrogant Europeans in the time of imperialism – a time when there were always also believers about: missionaries.

And finally I can't suppress the comment that even in this modern scientific parable we have just two *men*.

What has entered unconsciously into this parable is a view of the relationship between human beings and reality which is very one-sided but which nevertheless keeps cropping up.

I call it the jungle image of reality. Human beings come into a world full of confusion: they find order, meaning, connections, only as exceptions. That is often how we experience reality – in a pre-scientific way, in which life threatens to sink into chaos. But this is also our experience in the light of science. Don't we often feel lost in a giant cosmos of infinite dimensions – a tiny peripheral phenomenon on the surface of a tiny planet? The gypsies of the universe, we are surrounded by an infinitely great reality which is indifferent to our suffering, our pains and joys. We are aliens and intruders in a world which is really not our concern. We are illegal immigrants in it, without passports or residence permits, who have to make a home by force, wresting it from the jungle.

We can experience the world like this. We lack something if we can't. Indeed, we have to experience it like this. But that's not all. Human beings are not intruders into this garden. They are sons of the owner of the garden. It always belongs to him. Indeed human beings came into being through him. The plants and animals are their brothers and sisters. Not only Francis of Assisi says that. Science says it, too, except that it puts things in a cooler, more matter-of-fact way.

All life has the same genetic code. We are all part of one great stream of life. But only in human beings does it become conscious of itself. That raises us above all reality. Nevertheless we are part of the garden. Those who behave like intruders and imperialists in it are making exhibitions of themselves. We are sons and daughters of the gardener. That is certainly a rather poetic remark. But it fits our task in the world far better than the image of imperialistic intruders with electric fences and bloodhounds.

It is our task to do science in the spirit of the garden and the gardener, as a task which we do not impose on ourselves, but which we have always already found there first. All scientific activity must serve to preserve and tend the garden of the earth.

If that happens, we can also cope better with our anxieties in and about science: the anxieties of finitude, responsibility and the misuse of power.

If we act in the spirit of the gardener, we shall regard all our fragmentary knowledge as part of a dialogue – as a concern to respond to the task which we have been set. Involvement in this dialogue will become more important to us than the formulation of results. In a family the decisive thing is to keep talking, not always to find the best, the correct answers.

If we act in the spirit of the gardener, we shall be confident that this task can be coped with. The task may be very difficult, very complicated, perhaps insoluble for us. But in principle it can be solved. In other words, as Einstein put it, God is complicated but not malicious. And again there's a parallel with the family: if the parents show how life can be coped with, then a corresponding trust will grow up among the children.

Finally, anxiety about the misuse of the power of science. In the spirit of the gardener we shall be concerned to exert influence through knowledge. Knowledge is power – but that doesn't necessarily make it bad. The vital thing is for this power to be used in the spirit of the family. We must use this power to even things out between people. Or to keep to the image: we may discover that the garden has many different parts. Whole areas become deserts because no rain falls for years: in the Sahel, in Mozambique and Zimbabwe. The result is boundless misery: hunger, flight, disease. We can help. Not only by great economic programmes but by small gifts.

The decisive thing is for us to recognize that it is up to us how we use science. There is always the possibility of science becoming a science of barbed-wire fences, bloodhounds and electrified wires. If we use it in that way we shall neither find God nor serve God with it. But if we set out to tend our garden in the spirit of the gardener, because here we have a task, then we shall serve God with quite matter-of-fact scientific work. And participation in scientific thought can become a great piece of good fortune.

Then in scientific work, too, we will be able to experience that blessing with which I would like to end: May the peace of God which passes all our understanding keep your hearts and minds in Christ Jesus. Amen.

Unknowing Hope
A sermon against hopelessness

(Romans 8.18-26)

The theme of this sermon is hope. But the theme also has a counter-theme – hopelessness. For hope is either protest against a hopelessness which is consciously perceived, or an illusory wait for a better future.

In our papers these days we can see images of hopelessness: pictures from Cambodia, pictures of hungry, sick and apathetic people who are just waiting for death. In 1970 about seven million people lived in that country. Some fear that perhaps only three million will see the beginning of next year. Since the Holocaust, the most fearful crime in history known to us, this is the most abominable crime against humanity. It is happening now, at this moment, while we are gathered here for worship. It would be shameless to have a sermon on hope without having that before our eyes.

This is not just hopelessness caused by external events. The people of Europe also faced a heap of rubble at the end of the last world war. There was immeasurable suffering, of a kind that can hardly be imagined today. Nevertheless hope was alive. Why?

The answer isn't difficult to find: at that time it was easy to say that all the crimes had been caused by a barbaric and inhuman ideology which attached little importance to concealing its brutal features, but flaunted these openly. At that time we could say with good reason: if we begin from premises other than those of this barbaric ideology, we are safe from a repetition of this crime. Let us therefore build a society based on liberal values (as people said in Western Europe) or a society on a communist basis (as they said in Eastern Europe) – and then there will be hope for a just society and the overcoming of barbarity and crime. In addition, there was even the hope that religious conviction could be reactivated, leading to a renewal of individuals and society. At all events, there were clear alternatives to the criminal ideology and politics of German National Socialism.

Today in another situation we have no comparable alternatives to keep us from hopelessness. It was not the Nazis who dragged Cambodia into catastrophe. It was societies which had been formed by the great humane traditions on which resistance to National Socialism once drew. Liberal and communist societies share the blame for the catastrophe of Cambodia. And there is little point in blaming just particular variants of liberalism and communism. Thus it would be hypocrisy for us Europeans to accuse the American global ideology. For originally it was a European democracy which brought about the collapse in this region. First there was France's colonial war in Indo-China. And it is similarly pointless to blame just the Russian variants of communism. For ultimately the communists following China's lead destroyed the last hopes of peace. All the great humane traditions in politics failed; all the convictions on which we had set our hope after the last world war compromised themselves. There is no ideology, not a single one, which really furthered life. All perverted it.

And the religions? Their contribution wasn't very convincing. Both Buddhism and Christianity shaped Indo-China. There is certainly something in the hope that Buddhist meditation can contribute towards overcoming barbaric aggressiveness in us. But that doesn't alter the fact that incredible things happened in one of the homelands of Buddhism. And Christianity? I can well remember how many Christians were members of the Vietnamese government. And I recall the declarations of some of the American churches which supported the war (though certainly there were also many critical voices). But that doesn't help. We're all to blame. We all have reasons for being ashamed of ourselves. The ideas and convictions for which we argued were caught up in atrocities. There is no idea, no conviction, which can be claimed as a guarantee that we shall overcome need, war, hunger, anxiety and oppression.

In the last century people spent a long time discussing whether human beings were descended from animals or not. Many theologians insisted that hitherto a connecting link between primates

139

and *homo sapiens* had not been found – the famous 'missing link'. Nowadays, for many reasons we find it difficult to understand this discussion. One reason is our feeling that we ourselves are this missing link, the transitional stage between aggressive predators and cooperative human beings. Indeed, we must concede that everything which distinguishes us from the animals often only intensifies and stabilizes our aggressiveness. That is true above all of our frightening capacity to provide intelligent reasons why in some circumstances one may or even must kill other people.

Vietnam and Cambodia show that all the good ideas which we believe in can be misused to kill others, to drive them away, to deliver them over to hunger and sickness. All good ideas on which we have built our hope can result in hopelessness and suffering.

Is there hope nevertheless? The New Testament assures us that there is. Paul speaks of this hope in his letter to the Romans, chapter 8.14-26.

> *I consider that our present sufferings are not worth comparing with the glory that will be revealed in us. The creation waits in eager expectation for the sons of God to be revealed. For the creation was subject to frustration, not by its own choice, but by the will of the one who subjected it, in hope that the creation itself will be liberated from its bondage to decay and brought into the glorious freedom of the children of God. We know that the whole creation has been groaning as in the pains of childbirth right up to the present time. Not only so, but we ourselves, who have the firstfruits of the Spirit, groan inwardly as we wait eagerly for our adoption as sons, the redemption of our bodies.*

I love this text. It speaks of a great longing which is alive in everything: in the cosmos, in human beings, in the Spirit of God. It binds together nature, human beings and God. It points beyond the state in which we now find ourselves, as a threefold longing and a threefold sighing.

Let's begin with the longing of nature, with the 'groaning of creation' for redemption. In the Christian tradition we often find an abrupt contrast between human beings and nature. Many remarks in Paul are interpreted in this way. But here Paul stresses the opposite. Here he says that we belong together. Nature and human

140

beings correspond. The longing which takes hold of us when we are shattered by past and present suffering binds us to the whole of creation. It accords with a cosmic tendency. Every creature wants to get beyond pain and hurt; every creature presses on dully and unconsciously to develop its own life. Only in us human beings does this dull will become conscious of itself. Only we human beings bring this dumb sighing of the creation to consciousness. Only we deliberately follow a tendency that was already present before us. That is both consolation and encouragement. When hopelessness oppresses us, we should remember that human history is only a second in the evolution of the cosmos. Our history has only just begun. The infinitely great time-scale of cosmic history may often be oppressive. We seem to vanish in it. But it can also be encouraging. Human hope is something new in evolution. That also applies to the hope of Christians, communists and liberals. After such a short history as ours one can say, 'Two thousand years are too little to test this hope.' But it is understandable if sometimes we become sceptical. When such doubts overcome me, I think of the Neanderthals. At that time did anyone believe it possible that one day human beings could develop the technology and civilization which has in fact come about in the meantime? Such things were inconceivable then – in as much as we know anything about that time. But they happened. So precisely because of that we may not say that the hope of overcoming war and oppression is an illusion. Certainly it is a hope against all appearances, a hope against the reality of history so far and against conditions in our world. It is a hope against hope. But it is not a nonsensical hope. Much seems possible that we can now hardly imagine if we mark human history on the great evolutionary scale of the cosmos – if we regard our longing and hope as just one voice in the 'groaning of creation'.

However, our text speaks of more than this general hope. It speaks of the Christian hope that human beings – men and women – can become 'sons and children of God'. The term 'son of God' is originally a royal title. 'Sons of God' are distinguished by their sovereignty and freedom. They are no longer servants and slaves. That we should all achieve this royal sovereignty and freedom sounds like a daydream. But this daydream contains a criticism, namely the statement that we have not yet attained that sovereignty and freedom for which we are intended. We are still on the way to our destiny. As I John says, 'It is not yet manifest what we shall become' (3.1). Most people suspect nothing of this. Most people naively believe that we human beings are the cornerstone of creation and evolution and that there will be no essential development beyond us. This conviction is the expression of an ineradicable anthropocentric vanity: as though there had been a waiting time of twelve to sixteen billion years for *homo sapiens* to appear. But everything suggests that we are a transition. It is not yet manifest what we shall become. In Christianity we find a clear awareness of that. The New Testament says that we are a bridge to something new: we live between the old world and the new; we are a transition from animals to the true humanity which has not yet appeared. We ourselves are the 'missing link'. And we long for the new humanity to take form in us. We long to become sons and children of God. But Paul also says, 'All those who are impelled by the Spirit of God are now already God's sons.' In all Christians something is already alive now of what they will one day become. We are certainly on the way. But the Spirit which impels us is already part of the realization of what awaits us at the end.

Paul also speaks of a third longing, of the sighing, the 'groaning', of the Spirit. The Spirit comes to help our weakness. We do not know what we should pray for. We do not know what we long for. So the Spirit pleads for us with wordless sighs. The Spirit is the power which drives us on to become sons of God, which now already makes us free sons and children of God. This power is alive in the depths of our hearts, at a depth to which we ourselves do not see. Only God sees down to it. In this preconscious, unconscious and supra-conscious depth within human beings there springs up the longing to become sons and children of God. We detect this longing, but we do not know where it is driving us.

Not knowing is the decisive point as far as we are concerned. There are many groups which know precisely what the goal of human longing and human hope must look like. They know the recipe for the true human being. They know what the future to replace the present looks like. But as soon as they know that, they are inclined to divide human beings into two classes: those who correspond to this future and are on the way to it, and the others, the oppressors of true men and women, the enemies of the future, who stand in its way. It is a small step from this attitude to doing away with the enemies of the future, in order to realize a particular image of the new humanity. That is why it is important to keep stressing that we do not know the recipe for true humanity, We do not know what we are on the way to. We know that we are made in the image of God, but we may not make any image of God for ourselves. Nor may we draw a picture of his image – a blueprint by which we can create. We must keep saying, 'We don't know what we're hoping for – but we still hope.' We Christians cannot join in the cynical game of mocking socialist and liberal hopes because they have led to hopelessness and catastrophe. We Christians have sinned as much as everyone else, and our hopes have gone astray as much as everyone else's. We have reasons for being in solidarity with those whose hopes fail. We know that all hopes have their errors and their limitations. All hopes can be corrupted. There is no hope which cannot be used as a weapon of death. For that reason the best hope is the hope that knows just one thing: that we do not know what to long for. Such an un-knowing hope can never be used as an instrument for doing away with others. Such a hope can enable us to attempt to improve circumstances, but to do so in the awareness that these attempts are limited, part of a process of trial and error. Such unknowing hope can teach us to hope in a human way.

But if what we shall become is entirely open, what is this hope based on? Let me quote I John once again: 'Dear friends, now we are children of God, and what we will be has not yet been made known. But we know that when he appears, we shall be like him, for we shall see him as he is' (I John 3.2). He – that is Christ. The letter of John says that we know only one thing. It expressly uses the word 'know': we shall attain the state in which Christ already is. He is Son of God, and we are destined to become children of God. This hope is not based on our being initiated into God's plans, into the construction of the world and evolution. We have some inkling of that, but we do not know it. All we know is that in this gigantic universe – a mighty interplay of chance and necessity, of trial and error – it has proved possible to produce this one person. What was possible once is in principle possible again. So there is more in this universe than our sceptical hopelessness might suggest.

It's like a game of dice: you can have a long stretch of bad luck. But once a six comes up you know that the dice aren't rigged. There's a six there. It's come up once and it can come up again. There's the possibility of a lucky throw. It has happened in Jesus. Since him we can know that there is such a thing as a stroke of luck in the great universe – even if we don't quite understand the rules of the game, if we don't understand the player in whose hand we are. But his Spirit is in us. And he assures us with wordless sighs: 'You are destined to become free children of God – without anxiety and oppression.' This Spirit gives us peace, a peace which is beyond all our understanding. May this peace keep your hearts and minds in Jesus Christ. Amen.

Mourning at a Loss faced with Mass Graves
A sermon for a day of national mourning

(Romans 8.19-27)

Today is the Day of National Mourning, the penultimate Sunday before Advent, on which since 1952 we have thought of the fallen of both World Wars and the victims of National Socialism. Ever since I've been able to take a conscious part in this day, I've kept hearing a subsidiary theme in it: our doubt as to whether our mourning can in any way do justice to the events. Aren't we condemned to an 'inability to mourn' – partly because the shades of the past are so oppressive that no mourning can lighten them, and partly because we are not yet in a position to bid farewell to this past in mourning, to be able to face it freely.

By 'inability to mourn' I mean that our people is still in the position of a divorced spouse who has yet to find inward release from a failed relationship. Instead of breaking with it in mourning and grief, the spouse has been hurled into a new relationship – and all the unresolved problems of the past contribute to this new partnership.

To put it without the imagery: our people very rapidly dissociated itself from the compromised National Socialist ideals – so quickly, so uncannily quickly, that the parting could not be deepened by mourning and grief. We then enthusiastically took over new ideals from the humanitarian tradition of Western democracies, ideals which we had previously despised with arrogant feelings of superiority. But we transferred some things from the dark past into this new relationship. So our distancing of ourselves from Communism and the Soviet Union often became a substitute for the dissociation from National Socialism which everyone wanted: indeed it could be said that the basic anti-Soviet and anti-Communist mood of our society continued attitudes which had already played a sinister role in National Socialist Germany: many church people and Christians could affirm National Socialism at least as a 'bulwark' against atheistic Russia.

Let's be clear about it: inability to mourn doesn't mean the attitude of those who are always yesterday's people: it's the problem of those who have deliberately turned away from the past, who want to be different. It's our problem. We've mourned the loss of our former ideals too superficially. And our failure to do so is having its revenge. It's having its revenge in the verbal blunders of our politicians, which are all the more painful because they are quite superfluous to the thoughts of these politicians and run contrary to their declared intentions. If we had really said goodbye in pain and mourning to what the anti-Communist demagogery of Goebbels sought to tempt us into, no one would have thought of mentioning Goebbels and Gorbachev in the same breath.

Why is it so difficult to stand back from this past through mourning? Why are we still like a divorced spouse who remains inwardly bound to his or her former partner while hating that partner and rueing the day when the relationship came into being? Why is that true even for us younger ones? Whenever I go through the war cemetery in Heidelberg and read the names of the dead, and work out, 'He died at eighteen, he died at twenty, he died at twenty-two', a cold hatred and anger comes over me at the criminal policy of which these young men were the victims. And when I reflect that in the Rhineland I went to the same school as Goebbels and today teach at the very university at which he studied and gained his doctorate, I feel the shades of that crime reaching into my everyday life even now. Mustn't I ask myself whether those traditions which once shaped a Goebbels could also influence me? Did I perhaps have the same teachers as he did? Did I sit at the same desk? I can remember looking for J.G. among the names and initials carved on our desks – but in vain. Certainly such a desk would have been removed. Our school, too – with exceptions for which I am very grateful – practised that diplomatic silence about the past which became a characteristic of a large area of our political culture.

So are we condemned to an inability to mourn? No! We can mourn and we may mourn. At least that is what our text says, and

I want to us read it today as an invitation to mourning. Granted, it doesn't speak of mourning but of the threefold sighing, the threefold groaning, which goes through the world. It speaks of the groaning of all creation, the groaning of Christians and the groaning of the Spirit itself. Listen to these three voices as I read out the text.

The creation waits in eager expectation for the sons of God to be revealed. For the creation was subjected to frustration, not by its own choice, but by the will of the one who subjected it, in hope that the creation itself will be liberated from its bondage to decay and brought into the glorious freedom of the children of God. We know that the whole creation has been groaning in the pains of childbirth right up to the present time.

That is the first groaning, the groaning of all creation. From this in the following text Paul distinguishes the groaning of Christians. He continues:

Not only so, but we ourselves, who have the firstfruit of the Spirit, groan inwardly as we wait eagerly for our adoption as sons, the redemption of our bodies. For in this hope we were saved. But hope that is seen is no hope at all. Who hopes for what he already has? But if we hope for what we do not yet have, we wait for it patiently.

Paul then gives the groaning of Christians yet another new interpretation. It is the lamentation of God himself: the groaning of the Spirit. He writes:

In the same way, the Spirit helps us in our weakness. We do not know what we ought to pray for, but the Spirit himself intercedes for us with groans that words cannot express. And he who searches our hearts knows the mind of the Spirit, because the Spirit intercedes for the saints in accordance with God's will.

So our text speaks of a threefold sighing and groaning. It can give us three insights on this particular day.

1. Mourning is universal. We are not alone in our mourning.
2. The mourning of Christians does not take place without hope. It looks into the future.

3. We, too, do not know how to mourn as we should. No one knows that but God himself, who intercedes for us.

The first insight is that all creation mourns. Mourning is universal. It forms bonds, and does not separate. We should note that our mourning is not directed against anyone. Days of national mourning were often days of mourning against others; they could be misinterpreted as mourning against our former opponents in the Second World War – especially our opponents in the East, against nations which like the peoples of the Soviet Union had to mourn twenty million dead, and who in Hitler's plans were destined for slavery. Don't let's forget that of six million Russian soldiers who were prisoners of war, fifty-seven per cent died in our camps. In addition there was the suffering of the more than two million 'workers from the East' in Germany, who were also slaves in an inhuman regime.

A member of a church in the Ruhr described this. As a twenty-three year old young woman she was conscripted as a crane driver at the Hörder iron and steel works and her job was to teach Russian girls. It was strictly forbidden to give the starving workers from the East anything to eat. But each time she would leave something in the corner of the cab for the foreign girl. That came out. They suggested that she should blame the Russian girl: she had stolen it. But the crane driver acknowledged that she had given it voluntarily. She was ordered to beat the girl with a rubber truncheon. Again she refused. Finally the Russian girl was shut in a steel box as a punishment. The crane driver was ordered to lift this box on top of an oven, so that the girl would be subjected to intolerable heat. Yet again she refused. Confronted with the Gestapo she referred to the regulations: 'People may not be lifted with the crane.' She was told, 'But there was a Russian inside – they're not human.'

I've told this story to stress that our mourning must include all human beings. We must never say in retrospect, 'We'll leave out these victims. They're only Russians, only communists,' or whatever. Our mourning may not be mourning against others. For all sigh under the consequences of horrific human maltreatment, then and now.

We can derive a second insight from our text: our mourning takes place with a view to the future. Paul says that we are waiting for the revelation of a new humanity, for the appearing of the sons of God. In the New Testament human beings are regarded as transitional beings. They wait longingly to be changed. This change is already beginning now. Immediately before our text Paul confirmed this: those impelled by the Spirit of God are now already sons of God. They are now already the beginnings of that which all human beings are one day destined to be. And if anyone were now to ask me whether that was not an empty faith, I would refer to people like that crane driver. She and many others assure us that human beings who were capable of Auschwitz are called to something else. They reassure us that through all human aberrations, through terror and intimidation, sovereign signs of human solidarity keep breaking through which can give us courage.

Let me stress again, we need not mourn against others; but we must not mourn without hope. A third insight is equally important to me: we may concede to ourselves that we do not know how we should mourn – in a way that is fitting. In the face of millions of dead and immeasurable guilt there are no 'appropriate' attitudes, no acceptable interpretations; there is no mourning with a view to an end which one can achieve more or less effectively. We may concede that we are at a loss. I'm thinking of being at a loss in a very specific way. Of the victims of National Socialism and the German armies we can say: they died in the fight against evil or as victims of evil, as Jews, Poles, Sintis and Romas. But what about the millions of people who lost their lives as members of Hitler's armies? What about our fathers and uncles, our brothers? Isn't it a monstrous yet unavoidable thought that they died in battle for an abysmally evil system?

Here are the words of a combatant who was a resolute opponent of National Socialism and in 1950 returned from a Soviet prisoner-of-war camp:

Our present state of knowledge is a torment and burdens our memory of the millions of our fallen comrades. But on the whole they did not fight and did not die in the conviction that they were waging a war to impose slavery, one moreover which would utterly destroy the German Reich. Today I still mourn my younger brother, my fallen friends and comrades, who fought hard and with great dedication. And it is a terrrible thought that they lost their lives meaninglessly, indeed that they were even misused for criminal ends. If my grave was on the Waldai heights or by the Ilmensee and if – against all the odds – it was still recognizable, a passing Russian would probably murmur no more than, 'So there's the grave of yet another of that Fascist master race, those mass murderers.' And objectively speaking, would he be so wrong? How many thousands of the Soviet people were shattered, killed, mutilated by the shells which came from the artillery that I commanded? Or would perhaps a soft voice also say in this passer-by, 'Well, perhaps he too was just deceived'?

We might reflect how much would be achieved if the people against whom we once waged war could say, 'Perhaps many people too were just deceived?' Doesn't this, too, depend on our attitude? Isn't it up to us that the conviction is spread abroad that Germans are not necessarily military and aggressive, that Germans are not unteachable? Mustn't we shape our policies deliberately to communicate this message to all our neighbours? That wouldn't give the deaths of German soldiers a meaning after the event, but it would give a meaning to our life and our society today.

I grant that all these are helpless answers. And I also think that we should acknowledge our helplessness. We don't know how to mourn as we should. I don't know either. But precisely for that reason I derive a promise from Paul's words. Paul says, 'We do not know what we ought to pray for, but the Spirit himself intercedes for us with groans that words cannot express.'

We may allow ourselves to be at a loss, to give way to pain, at the catastrophes caused by human and German guilt, confident that God's Spirit is at work in this grief. God himself mourns in us with a groaning which cannot be expressed. God himself mourns in his creatures who are at a loss – and takes their part, despite all their guilt and despite all their inability to accept it and assimilate it. In conceding that we are helpless as we mourn, we come nearer to God than through the claim that we have made up for the past guilt of our fathers. By conceding that we are still confused, wounded and disorientated when we think of the dead of the World Wars and the victims of National Socialism, we come closer to these dead, these victims, than through the over-hasty proclamation that we have now learned the lesson of history. Over many years and many abysses, however, one thing unites us with those many dead who died as dupes: they looked on helplessly as a criminal regime established itself, and they became increasingly deeply entangled in it. We often look helplessly back – and cannot cope with the consequences of this criminal regime any more than they could with its heralds.

If in this way we join company with those who were led astray, just as we join company with their victims, then today we can understand the text like this. We do not know how to mourn. We are at a loss. But we are not alone in this mourning. It is in harmony with the lamentation of every tormented creature. It is in harmony with the mourning of God in his creatures. We are woven into a harmony of mourning. And precisely at that point God is near. For the God of whom the Bible speaks did not keep away from suffering, pain and mourning. He himself entered the sphere of conflict and death. He is to be found not only in the beauty of creation, but also and particularly in the crucified Jesus, in guilt and death.

All of us, the dead and the living, are dependent on his forgiving our guilt. Only because of that can we say that the dead rest in his peace. Only because of that may I give you, the living, the blessing of his peace. May this peace of God which passes all our understanding keep your hearts and minds in Christ Jesus. Amen.

Preparation for the Journey into an
Unknown Land
On coming to terms with death

———

(II Corinthians 1.1-11)

The text for this sermon comes at the beginning of the second letter to the Corinthians. We shall hear it differently if we know Paul's situation when he was writing this letter to Corinth, the capital of Achaea, from Ephesus. There Paul had just survived a situation in which his life had been in danger. He was quite sure that a trial would end in a death sentence for him, but contrary to his expectation he had been acquitted.

It is equally important that Paul was writing after a serious conflict with the Corinthian community. He had been deeply hurt during a brief visit there – we don't know the precise details. But now the community had indicated its readiness for reconciliation.

So we are listening to the words of an apostle who is happy to have been saved from the danger of death and is being reconciled with other people. The disaster which was threatening from inside and outside the community has been averted. He writes:

Paul, an apostle of Christ Jesus by the will of God, and Timothy our brother, To the church of God in Corinth, together with all the saints throughout Achaea: Grace and peace to you from God our Father and the Lord Jesus Christ.

Praise be to the God and Father of our Lord Jesus Christ, the Father of compassion and the God of all comfort, who comforts us in all our troubles, so that we can comfort those in any trouble with the comfort we ourselves have received from God. For just as the sufferings of Christ flow over into our lives, so also through Christ our comfort overflows. If we are distressed, it is for your comfort and salvation; if we are comforted, it is for your comfort, which produces in you patient

152

endurance of the same sufferings we suffer. And our hope for you is firm, because we know that just as you share in our sufferings, so also you share in our comfort. We do not want you to be uninformed, brothers, about the hardships we suffered in the province of Asia. We were under great pressure, far beyond our ability to endure, so that we despaired even of life. Indeed, in our hearts we felt the sentence of death. But this happened that we might not rely on ourselves but on God, who raises the dead. He has delivered us from such a deadly peril, and he will deliver us. On him we have set our hope that he will continue to deliver us, as you help us by your prayers. Then many will give thanks on our behalf for the gracious favour granted us in answer to the prayers of many.

Paul has looked death in the face. He has learned something in the process which is also valuable for others. So he is sharing it in his letter. It's not just intended for the few who, like him, find themselves in the situation of martyrdom. It's important for all of us. For all of us carry around a death sentence within us. It's inscribed on every living being. It's ciphered in the code of life. But only we human beings can decipher this verdict. Only we know that we have to die, though we don't know when, where and how.

Christian preaching has a duty to read this verdict and continually spell it out anew. Passiontide is a time of *memento mori*. However, recollection of death seems as unmodern a conscious experience of this springtime as Passiontide. Nevertheless, we should recall death – for the sake of life.

Among the controversial sketches for the windows of the Holy Spirit Church there is an impressive variation on *memento mori*: the depiction of an electrocardiogram. Here we read in modern cypher the message 'life is finite'. First of all we see the excited heartbeats of an embryo. Then the heartbeats of a dying person gradually fading away. And in the middle, between the symbolic language of the medical apparatus which accompanies our being born and our dying, the time-span which is allotted to us. In a conversation about these sketches, a scientist who is professionally occupied with life every day said to me, 'Isn't that a sad message? Shouldn't the church be saying something positive?' I retorted, 'What else can the church say if it may no longer proclaim a *memento mori* all over the world? Is the tabu of silence over death also to prevail in the church?'

On the other hand it is beyond dispute that everyone is preoccupied with dying and death. Books on death sell well: books on separation, mourning, personal experience in dying, reports of those who were clinically dead and came to life again. But this interest is no contradiction of the tabu over death. For this interest draws its power precisely from the fact that death is tabu. What do people maintain an embarrassed silence about in everyday life? What kind of an event is it which is bracketted off from the commercial world and its promises of happiness for all walks of life? At most it appears in the advertising of some life assurance companies, who tell us: 'You must plan for the worst case, that you'll live to ninety.' What is it that embarrasses modern theologians?

Christian recollection of death nowadays has to struggle with two difficulties. Christian preaching is still constantly accused of having for centuries regarded this life as simply a preparation for another life. Certainly an approach which regards the whole of life as a preparation for dying seems hostile to human beings – and in addition neglects life. And if the message of the church was once, 'There is a life after death', now it often runs, 'There is a life before death.' However, we should judge past preaching fairly. The first question of the Heidelberg Catechism is not, 'What is your only comfort in dying?', but, 'What is your only comfort in *living* and dying?'

A second reason why the *memento mori* has fallen so silent in the Christian church may be rather different: dying and death are an abyss of suffering and pain. And we ask ourselves whether we have the right to tear open this abyss if at the same time we can't point to a hand which preserves us there. But people hardly believe the church with its message that death is not the last word. Most people feel that we are on a journey into the utterly unknown – and who is not anxious about this journey?

You know the question, 'What would you take with you if you could have three things on a desert island?' How about three items of luggage for the journey into the unknown? What items from our Christian faith would we choose for this journey? I propose to take three items from our text to go with us on our journey.

Now of course someone will object that this is a journey on which no one can take anything. Everything will be taken away from us.

Even we ourselves will be taken away from ourselves. I grant that I can cover only the journey to the frontier. Beyond that is a great unknown land. We don't even know that the brash statement that everything ends with death holds. That, too, is unknown.

But our journey already begins here. It begins every day. The three items of luggage that we take with us are already to be of use here, in the midst of life, not just when it comes to an end – not just at the periphery. Paul, too, isn't writing at the periphery. He's just had life restored to him. He's experienced a great success: reconciliation with his community is beginning. He's a happy man.

Because of that I also want to avoid steeping your imagination in the terror of dying. I want to avoid dwelling on cancer, on intensive care, on casualty wards. I'm certain that you all know that dying and death are an abyss of pain and grief (and that a gentle death is a blessing). And because we all know this, I needn't conjure it up for long.

Let's ask, rather, 'What three items of luggage from our Christian faith would we take with us on our journey?'

Paul writes that he despaired of life. He had firmly expected death because 'we might not rely on ourselves but on God, who raises the dead'. In another text he also speaks of trust in God who calls nothing into being. And for me that is the first thing that we need on our journey: trust in the power which creates being out of nothing. This power already surrounds us now. It surrounds us every moment. It always surrounded us. It's just that we don't notice it. The enigma of death is neither greater nor smaller than the whole enigma of our existence.

It's quite useful for Christians to develop a philosophical bent at this point. For it's around this enigma that the age-old philosophical questions are grouped. Why is there anything at all? Why do I exist? Why this mysterious bond to this one life? What is the enigmatic present other than the passing frame of a film which in both directions fades into nothingness? The past is no more. The future is not yet. The present is a transition. I can't solve any of these riddles. Perhaps, too, that's not the meaning of these mysteries which surround us on all sides. Perhaps it isn't a matter of developing a few new ideas about the world in which these mysteries are also explained. Perhaps it's more a matter of how we lead our lives in accord with this

mystery. We are questioned. And where we know that we are
questioned in this way, the voice of God touches our life, the voice
which asks us, 'Adam, where are you?'

We often ignore this voice. It's often soft. Other voices are louder.
But sometimes it breaks through everything. Sometimes we're
overwhelmed by the fact that our life and all being is a miracle which
we ourselves have not performed. Sometimes it's in situations like
those Paul experienced, sometimes when we receive a diagnosis
from the doctor which indicates that our suspicion of a serious illness
was unfounded. Or when we just escape an accident. Or in happy
experiences: when we feel that someone else finds it quite wonderful
that we exist and are there. Every day we can trace something of
that power which has snatched us from nothingness and holds us
over it. Then we can say with Matthias Claudius:

> I thank God and rejoice
> like a child over a Christmas gift
> that I am. That I am, and you
> have a beautiful human face.

That above all is something that we should take with us on our
journey into an unknown land, and already we should be practising
every day a sense of the miracle of being. The mystery of being and
nothingness – the mystery of creation – surrounds us every moment
in life, and our journey leads into this mystery. That is why Christian
preaching doesn't say 'There is a life after death'. It says, first and
foremost, 'There is a life before death, a life in the mystery of God.
In death we all fall back into this mystery.'

Perhaps that's still too abstract for some people. So let me choose
a second item from Christian faith for our journey into the great
unknown. When Paul says that we put our trust in God who raises
the dead, he means the God who raised Jesus from the dead. In
Christ we are encountered concretely by the power which calls
nothingness into being and surrounds our being on all sides. Paul
feels near to this power in all dangers, but also in all happiness. A
little later he writes in his letter: 'We carry the death of Jesus around
in our body, so that the life of Jesus may also be visible in our body.'

However, now someone could say, 'But the resurrection of Jesus
is so problematical. Who knows what happened? First of all the

sources have to be interpreted, and there are many opinions about them. I don't want to get into all that. You can have a relationship to Jesus without sorting out the resurrection.'

I mean something very simple. On our journey into an unknown land we have a companion, Jesus. He is already our companion in life. He is already our companion through a wonderful land in which the birds of the air and the lilies of the field give us courage to live. He doesn't promise us that the end of the journey will be easy. Before his death he trembled with anxiety, and wanted to escape death. His death was a torment. We may know that wherever the journey leads, we are where Jesus is. When we hear of his Easter appearances they may just seem like a sheet of lightning in a dark night. We don't know where it comes from and how we should interpret it. But if we've lived in communion with Jesus – not only at the end of life but in the midst of it – we can be sure that in communion with him we experience something that no death can destroy – even if it escapes our concepts and images.

I find that expressed in a restrained way in a letter which Klaus Bonhoeffer wrote in March 1945, after he had been condemned to death for his involvement in the rebellion against Hitler. He wrote this from prison to his daughter Cornelia:

All the winter sparrows have been visiting my window-sill. Now a thrush is already singing outside, morning and evening. The catkins that Mama brought me are standing on my table. After the unpleasant winter, perhaps for the first time you will rightly be enjoying the spring. Just open your eyes and see how everything is beginning imperceptibly to stir. That's the mysterious time. Then suddenly, new life, joy and new courage also come over us with power. Take what comes and enjoy it with a glad heart. It's a gift from heaven...

Here Mama is now visiting me once a week, and every day she sends some food to my cell with a lovely greeting. I hope that you too will be as brave and firm in faith, even in the most difficult times...

Now good-bye, my dearest Cornelia. Pray that God will give us strength in need. It's good that you're also reading the Psalms. You'll also have read the bitter passion story and about Easter

Day. Warmest greetings to Aunt L. Lots of love to you, Thomas and Walter, from Papa.

How good it would be if we too could talk like that! In the shadow of the bitter passion story and Easter Day there is a life before death – which withstands even death. It is a life which is full of tenderness towards this life – which also perceives the sparrows in the sky and the willow catkins in the field as a sign of grace. It is a life in communion with Jesus. This closeness to Jesus is the second item that we need on our journey to the unknown land of death.

Now we need a third item to take with us. The first was trust in the creative power of God. The second was the closeness of Jesus as a companion in living and dying. The third item isn't difficult to guess, since this sermon is built on the three articles of faith: it must have something to do with the Holy Spirit, with the Spirit which binds all Christians. In his first letter to the Corinthians Paul wrote that those who possess the Spirit form one body. And he concludes from that: 'So if one member suffers, all the members suffer with it; if one member is honoured, all the others rejoice with it.' Now, in the second letter to the Corinthians, he has occasion to apply this image to himself and the community. He has been in deadly danger. Suppose that he had been executed in Ephesus at that time. It would have been a doubly bitter death. Paul would have died unreconciled with his community, offended, hurt, feeling that he had been wrongly treated – not only by his judges but by his friends in Corinth. The Corinthian community could not have heard of his death without guilt feelings. It's bitter to say good-bye to one's fellow human beings unreconciled – for both the dying and the living. That's the background to Paul's words in our text: 'He (God) comforts us in all our troubles, so that we can comfort those in any trouble with the comfort we ourselves have received from God... If we are distressed, it is for *your* comfort and salvation; if we are comforted, it is for *your* comfort... We know that just as you share in our sufferings, so also you share in our comfort.' This comfort consists in the fact that Paul and the Corinthians have been given the chance of reconciliation.

That's not to be taken for granted. On the contrary. Here the human spirit tends more towards the attitude which we meet in the anecdote of the old farmer.

> A pastor told a terminally ill old farmer that he should be reconciled with the neighbour who had become his enemy, since his last hour was approaching. The old fool found it difficult to give the pastor permission to bring the neighbour round to be reconciled. And even when he had given his consent, he still wasn't finished with the matter. He called after the pastor, 'But if I get better, things with Matthew will go back to what they were.'

Our spirit is pre-programmed to live life as a struggle against other life. And if we come together, it is above all so as to be able to carry on this fight more effectively. Even death often seems to us to be a crafty way for evolving life constantly to begin again, so that development can take place through fortuitous changes caused by the succession of generations and an unfair distribution of chances for life and survival. But we human beings have taken an irreversible step into new territory, a step which we take and feel in this life: in us life's quarrel with itself becomes conscious – and can be overcome. We can experience all being as something that is bound up with us. And we can understand all life as an ally against death. We can be taken hold of by the Spirit of reconciliation and be changed. For this spirit is rebellion against life's quarrel with itself, a rebellion in the midst of this life. God himself gives us encouragement: Be reconciled!

I've looked out three items to take on the great journey into the unknown: God's nearness, in our astonishment at the mystery of being; Jesus' nearness, as companionship in living and dying; and the nearness of the Spirit, as a way of overcoming enmity and division. But you will ask, 'May we take them all with us? Won't they be taken away from us at the frontier?'

I want to end with an illustration. Perhaps we're like addicts who find a welcome in a group of fellow-addicts – in a group which seeks a way out of dependence and self-destruction by working on themselves and helping one another. I heard from one such group that they had a remarkable membership ceremony which can be understood only by those who know how hard the break with the old life required of an addict is.

New members have to stand in the middle of a circle formed by the group, close their eyes, and let themselves fall backwards. They're assured, 'We'll catch you.' But as yet the person in the centre doesn't know any of the group. He or she has to trust strangers. Any request for a mattress to be put down on the floor first – to prevent anxiety – is refused. One day the new member must take the step into the unknown and trust an entirely strange environment.

For us death is like that. We can't try it out. We can't reassure ourselves in advance about what comes afterwards. We're accepted into it only once. But we're already saved now – in the midst of life – when we show that trust which allows us to fall backwards, blind, without knowing the hands that will receive us. We're already saved now – in life before death – when we trust that we shall not make a hard landing but are safe – safe in a peace which even now can make our hearts light and which passes all our understanding. May this peace of God keep your hearts and minds, in living and dying, in Jesus Christ. Amen.

The End of the Compulsion to Sacrifice
On the sacrificial death of Jesus

(Hebrews 10.1-18)

The law is only a shadow of the good things that are coming – not the realities themselves. For this reason it can never, by the same sacrifices repeated endlessly year after year, make perfect those who draw near to worship. If it could, would they not have stopped being offered? For the worshippers would have been cleansed once and for all, and would no longer have felt guilty for their sins. But those sacrifices are an annual reminder of sins, because it is impossible for the blood of bulls and goats to take away sins.

Therefore, when Christ came into the world, he said:

'Sacrifice and offering you did not desire,
but a body you prepared for me;
with burnt offerings and sin offerings you were not pleased.
Then I said, "Here I am – it is written about me in the scroll –
I have come to do your will, O God." '

First he said, 'Sacrifices and offerings, burnt offerings and sin offerings you did not desire, nor were you pleased with them' (although the law required them to be made). Then he said, 'Here I am, I have come to do your will.' He sets aside the first to establish the second. And by that will, we have been made holy through the sacrifice of the body of Jesus Christ once for all.

Day after day every priest stands and performs his religious duties: again and again he offers the same sacrifices, which can never take away sins. But when this priest had offered for all time one sacrifice for sins, he sat down at the right hand of God. Since that time he waits for his enemies to be made his footstool, because by one sacrifice he has made perfect for ever those who are being made holy. The Holy Spirit also testifies to us about this. First he says:

'This is the covenant I will make with them
after that time,' says the Lord.

161

'I will put my laws in their hearts,
and I will write them on their minds.'

Then he adds:

'Their sins and lawless acts
I will remember no more.'

And where these have been forgiven, there is no longer any sacrifice
for sin.

At Passiontide the following story often goes through my head. In a pastor's family the parents were looking at picture books with their six-year-old son. Among the pictures was one of the crucified Jesus. On seeing it the son protested. He didn't want to look at this picture. Why? 'I hate this God,' he explained. His parents were startled. What was up? 'I hate this God,' the child explained, 'because he kills his son.'

We should take this child seriously. Doesn't he say openly what we repress? Isn't the sacrifice of the Son by the Father based on an archaic mystery? Freud thought that he had deciphered it. The sacrificial death of the Son expresses the repressed conflict of all human beings with their parents. It represents the defeat of the rebel Son, and his exaltation to the right hand of the Father represents his secret victory. Freud thought that this myth went back deep into the forgotten primal times of individual and collective life and spoke of a 'family drama' which each of us has undergone. That is why the myth has such fascination for us.

Earliest Christianity speaks of the sacrificial death of Jesus differently. For Christianity this death is not the echo of a repressed primal time, but a step forwards. For centuries human beings had sacrificed to idols. It was impossible to think of worship of God without bloody sacrifices. Now that was to come to an end. Now a revolution was to take place in the history of religion. Jews, Christians and some philosophers developed forms of religion without sacrifice. That was a radical break with the past.

This break came about for Jews through the destruction of the temple and for Christians through the sacrificial death of Christ. The unique sacrifice brings freedom from many sacrifices. That is the message of the letter to the Hebrews. It says that it is liberating not to have to sacrifice any more. We would understand if it said that it is liberating not to have to keep on sacrificing – always having to give without receiving anything in return. Many of us know this compulsion to sacrifice. However, the text is not speaking of self-sacrifice but of bloody animal sacrifices, of the sacrifice of other life. Only if we have some idea of why people kept sacrificing animals can we understand why freedom from this compulsion to sacrifice was so liberating. But the ancient texts about sacrifice don't tell us very much. They are sacrificial rituals, instructions for priests about what they should do. They say nothing about the significance of the event. The killing of animals is done without interpretation, and their burning takes place in silence. Even the cheerful meal after the killing does not convey anything about the significance of the sacrifice. The sacrificial practice of ancient peoples is as alien to us as the rituals of an ant colony. We're thrown back on our own interpretations as observers.

Let's attempt such an interpretation. Every sacrifice has two aspects: on the one hand it is a gift for the benefit of others, God and the community, an act of solidarity. On the other it is annihilation and destruction: an aggressive act. We make use of both aspects of sacrifice. We speak of sacrificial giving for the needy. And we speak of those who are sacrificed, the victims of a dictatorship or a terrorist attack. We shall be reflecting on both aspects of sacrifice today: as an act of solidarity and as an act of aggression.

Nowadays there is often talk of 'sacrificial solidarity'. The context of this slogan is an embittered struggle over distribution in our society, above all over the distribution of work, and particularly meaningful work. To make work possible for all, sacrificial solidarity is called for. But everyone is afraid that a 'special sacrifice' will be asked of them. So everyone is on their guard against that.

Here the story of a harmless theatre fire occurs to me – at a time when there were no modern safety curtains. Fire had broken out on the stage. Everyone was rushing to the exit. But the door opened inwards. Everyone was asked to take a step back. But no one did – impelled by their own fears for their lives and pushed by others. The door remained shut. The fire on the stage was put out. But some people died in the human crush nevertheless. It's the same with us: if we were ready for everyone to take one step back, we could open the door towards solving the problem of unemployment. But in our anxiety that we might get less than our fair share, boxed into our interest groups, we push in the wrong direction. That's human, but nevertheless it's deeply shaming. It's shaming that we can't do the obvious: at least share burdens between the generations, between those who have work and those who have none. If everyone simply gave up half their Christmas money, one new job could be created for every fifty. But even this moderate suggestion of a small sacrifice (and it was the suggestion of a prime minister in office) found no hearing in the land of the brave and successful.

Sacrifices are always associated with struggles over distribution. That also applied to sacrifices in ancient societies. When someone offered the first-fruits of his harvest, when he brought the fattest calves for the sacrificial meal, he was demonstrating publicly that despite personal success he had not forgotten the community. There is an element of avoiding envy here. Those who have possessions attract the envy of those who do not. The sacrifice mitigates the envy. Even the richest person must give something to the gods. Social envy is projected on to the gods: they would be cross if they didn't get anything; if they didn't get fat to smell and if the aroma of burning flesh didn't ascend – in practical terms, if priests and the sacrificing community didn't get anything. All sacrifices are sacrifices of solidarity in the struggle over the distribution of opportunities in life – born of anxiety about envy and guilt-feelings towards others. So one can be sympathetic towards people who thought that the world and society would collapse without sacrifices, that without sacrifice the envy of the gods would destroy people.

But the first Christians said, 'We're free from this compulsion to sacrifice. We don't have to propitiate any envious gods who want to have their fair share. We don't have to compel those with possessions to perform a symbolic act of subordination to society through sacrifical obligations. No, God himself sacrifices his Son. And the Son who is sacrificed does not remain in death. His sacrifice supercedes sacrifices.' So Christians ceased offering bloody sacrifices. Among Christians the place of sacrifices was taken by the eucharist. At its centre stands the sharing of food: the breaking of one bread and the drinking of the common cup. In the Christian eucharist the sharing of material possessions is made something holy. In it God is present. We rightly see the significance of the eucharist endangered when this notion of community is violated, when someone is excluded. For God cannot be present in the eucharist unless each neighbour can be present in it.

But that has consequences: you can't experience God's presence in the sharing of bread and wine and refuse the sharing of material opportunities in society. You can't break bread here with some and withhold bread there from others.

All sacrifices are sacrifices of solidarity, including the one sacrifice of Christ which is recalled in the eucharist. It assures us that we may allow ourselves to be given gifts – this life and all that makes it beautiful – without being afraid that this is an illegitimate theft. And we may give away these riches without being anxious about going short. Both anxieties, anxiety that we are taking something away from others and anxiety about going short, were once banished in archaic sacrificial transactions. Freed from this anxiety, Christians no longer need a sacrifice.

However, sacrifices aren't only sacrifices in solidarity; they are also aggressive actions. Sacrificing animals is killing. For centuries acts of killing stood at the centre of religions. We must also reflect on this gloomier side of sacrifice.

The term we use for an animal sacrifice is victim. We too speak of victims of catastrophes and road accidents. By using this image of the victim we are indicating that these victims died vicariously for us, 'vicariously' in the simple sense that the same thing could also have happened to us. In statistical terms, each year we condemn a certain number of people to death by the existence of our road systems. Any of us could be the next victim.

But we speak of 'victims' not only in connection with unmerited suffering but also in connection with culpable misdemeanours. Then we need 'scapegoats' and send people out into the wilderness – although only a few are aware that in so doing we are alluding to a biblical ritual. On the Day of Atonement two he-goats were sacrificed. One was for Yahweh; the other was driven out into the wilderness bearing the sins of the people, to perish there. Our democratic order is based on such a scapegoat ritual: every four years we choose our politicians – and four years later send them out into the wilderness if they are no use. Sometimes scandals lead to that earlier, if misdemeanours, corruption and shady dealings become too rife. Sometimes we get the impression that this ritual is no longer functioning with the impact to be desired. At all events it has archaic features. Discontent piles up, tensions arise, and so the public looks for a scapegoat. Away with him! But beyond doubt the ritual serves as a purification: it gives the chance of a new beginning. Everyone explicitly acknowledges those norms and values which have been violated.

The animal victims of the ancient world also had this purifying function. Perhaps it was primaeval hunters who invented animal sacrifices as a preparation for the hunt: for it is necessary on the one hand to incite the 'hunt's joyful lust for murder' (as Goethe put it) and on the other hand to see that the lust for murder is not directed against fellow hunters, but only against animals. So people kill an animal together, direct the aggression to a sacrifice and thus – at the cost of the one sacrifice – salvage the cohesion of the group. Here the Old Testament scapegoat brings out an aspect which is part of any sacrifice.

We still haven't got beyond such scapegoat rituals. On the contrary, today we're experiencing a revival of anti-Jewish prejudices or, to be more precise, a revival of the expression of such prejudices. There are developments here in our society which worry us, which cause tension, for example the destruction of housing areas by property speculators. And again as a result a minority is being attacked of which at most ten per cent are involved in this development.

How good it would be if the message of Hebrews were true, that through the one sacrifice the many sacrifices have become superfluous, that through the one scapegoat the many scapegoats have been spared! This message has not yet reached the hearts of all Christians. And yet it is a great message: in the New Testament Jesus himself takes the role of the outsider, the persecuted, the scapegoat. In so doing he gives us an opportunity to see through and do away with scapegoat complexes. For this scapegoat is different. The Old Testament scapegoat was sent into the wilderness, there to perish with the sins of the people. It was to take with it the tensions of society. It was to be blotted out with them. But Jesus takes over the role of the scapegoat to break through these tensions. He returns. He, the outsider, becomes the centre of a new society. He, the sacrificial victim, becomes the high priest. He, the condemned man, becomes the judge. The impotent one becomes ruler of the worlds. The one who is killed does not remain dead but continues to live in the hearts of all believers.

By interpreting the death of Jesus with sacrificial imagery, with the images of the scapegoat and the sacrificial lamb, the New Testament sets out to indicate that everything that those who sacrificed once sought with the help of their sacrifices they now find in Christ. And so there is no longer a compulsion to sacrifice, to sacrifice life in order to ensure one's own survival. There is no compulsion to create outsiders in order to consolidate one's own position. The sacrifice of Christ fulfils all the archaic needs that in the past drove human beings to sacrifice. It fulfils the need for solidarity and wards off destructive envy. It fulfils the need for common aggression against others through whom groups consolidate their cohesion. Here we should think of the eucharist: we celebrate it as communion with one who was a despised outsider, who was driven out as a scapegoat. He is the centre of our community. Therefore our community must measure itself by the way in which it deals with outsiders and minorities. In the midst of the struggle over the distribution of opportunities, the eucharist bears witness to a life which does not live at the expense of other life.

So what do we say to that six-year-old pastor's son who was shocked when he looked at a crucifixion scene? What should we say when he asks, 'Why did God sacrifice his Son? Is God cruel?' We should tell him that God sacrificed him to free us from the compulsion to sacrifice. He reversed the sacrifice of the Son when he called the crucified Jesus back to life and made the condemned man the judge. He wanted to tell us, 'Give up bloody sacrifices. I have already ensured that you will find what you seek with your sacrifices: true life.' So we have the promise that we shall become free from the compulsion to sacrifice, and thus experience the peace of God which passes all understanding. May this peace keep your hearts and minds in Christ Jesus. Amen.

Criteria for a Living Faith
Or, On the courage to live and die

(Revelation 3.1-6)

To the angel of the church in Sardis write: 'These are the words of him who holds the seven spirits of God and the seven stars. I know your deeds; you have a reputation of being alive, but you are dead. Wake up! Strengthen what remains and is about to die, for I have not found your deeds complete in the sight of my God. Remember, therefore, what you have received and heard; obey it, and repent. But if you do not wake up, I will come like a thief, and you will not know at what time I will come to you.

Yet you have a few people in Sardis who have not soiled their clothes. They will walk with me, dressed in white, for they are worthy. He who overcomes will, like them, be dressed in white. I will never blot out his name from the book of life, but will acknowledge his name before my Father and his angels. He who has an ear, let him hear what the Spirit says to the churches.'

There is an aggressive statement in our text. It was once applied to the church in Sardis. Now it is addressed to us. The sense of it is: 'You only seem to be alive; in reality you're dead!'

Many people say that today about the Christian churches. Many young people looking for more intense experiences in religion are repelled by our services because of their impression of people sitting there with long faces, and hymns attuned to the beyond in a cultural ruin from ancient times which one can respectfully visit but not live in.

'You only seem to be alive, but you're dead.' That is said by some students of theology. Once a spark was struck in their lives, the recognition that between cradle and grave the most important thing is to be clear about the one thing needful: about God and goodness, about life, justice and love. They think that all theological reflection ought to be aglow with these questions. But they don't detect any of that in the moving around of ideas and concepts, texts and words. They find our scholarly learning an empty activity, which only seems to be alive.

'You only seem to be alive, but you're dead.' That's what the pious man or woman, the person whose faith is secure in a personal relationship to God, says to today's church. Such people perceive little of this faith in the Christian community: anxiety and doubt are cultivated there. Beguiling fascination with one's own suffering is often greater among Christians than fascination with God's creation and the life that we have been given. Isn't such a community dead?

'You only seem to be alive, but you're dead.' That is said by Christians to whom the security of our life has become a problem when they think of the many people who hunger and thirst after bread and righteousness. How can one live peacefully as a disciple of Jesus knowing that we are all hurled into an inexorable struggle over the distribution of opportunities between peoples, social systems and classes? Chance has put us on the side of the privileged. Our secure life is life at the expense of others, life which lives from the deaths of others.

On all sides we hear critical voices. 'You only seem alive, in reality you're dead.' We often disappoint anyone in search of a living church. It doesn't matter whether such people understand by a living church an experience of fellowship or a partisan group sworn to produce a more just world; whether they are looking for a centre for a deep and secure faith or a place of spiritual clarity about the basic questions of life. From all sides the critical questions come to us: 'Where's your life? Your vigour? Aren't you dead?'

Today we're going to listen to another voice – a voice which we hear in this text, a voice which gives a criterion for life and death. This criterion is simple and clear. The sign of life in a community is that it remains steadfast in conflicts over the divinization of those with earthly power and does not blur the difference between God and human beings. That it is a community to which this is so important that it is prepared to accept persecution and death. That is the situation of the community in the Revelation of John.

It's not our situation. The courage of martyrs isn't required of us.

We may welcome the fact that many Christians nowadays are taking sides at great personal sacrifice in the controversies over arming and disarming. There can be no question of martyrdom here. Here in the framework of a democratic society there is the perception of a guaranteed basic right of opposition. Here civil disobedience is practised. To call this 'resistance' is already to put it too high, and the word 'martyrdom' would be the wrong label.

And yet we can learn from our text. The situation of martyrdom can come about at any time. No one should feel safe. This situation comes as unexpectedly as a thief in the night. Anyone who isn't ready and watching is unprepared for it. So even now it has to be said loudly and clearly:

Christian faith is courage to live and die – even to die for one's own convictions. Theological talk about the unconditional is abstract and pale. What it is really about is that which is of unconditional concern, that which we would not betray in any circumstances – not even if we could save our lives by doing so. Christian faith is alive if it's clear about that.

So what makes a living community? Not a community experience, nor commitments to justice, spiritual clarity and secure faith by themselves. A community is alive when it emanates this courage to live and die. It is alive when it bears witness to this courage in all the expressions of its life: in its worship and its hymns, in its theological reflection and spirituality.

So let's ask, 'What gives us courage to live and die?'

Perhaps you're the same as me. When I let my thoughts wander, pictures emerge of happy times – of times in which one renews the covenant with life. Everyone has a different picture. I can envisage, for example, a small lake in Scandinavia, my children in a boat gliding over the water, birch trees glittering in the sun. And I slowly repeat the words of Yahweh from the beginning of the Bible: 'And behold, it was very good.' For a moment it's as though creation has succeeded. Courage to live and die is based on such simple experiences – on the experience that the world isn't completely absurd and recalcitrant, but is God's good creation.

But that can't be all. For this original courage will inexorably land in a crisis. This courage is crucified and buried in life. It experiences the unavoidable defeats of life – even if no great catastrophes come.

All human beings are bound to their bodies – once and for all. They all experience their limits here in sickness and death.

At some point we all always experience situations of injustice which hurt and are painful for a long time.

Everyone always at some point encounters someone for whose love he or she would give everything – but the other escapes them.

Everyone at some point stakes everything on doing well at something – and has to be content with coming last or next to last.

There are enough crisis situations in normal everyday life – long before the great trial of martyrdom, from which may God preserve us. In these situations Christian faith proves itself – as courage to live and die which is shaped by encounter with the figure of Christ.

Here's a rather trivial illustration to show what I mean. When I'm uncertain about how to judge academic work and already feel tempted perhaps to be more lenient than my own conviction dictates, I see in my mind's eye my teacher shaking his head – and then I do what I think right. That's only a fairly trivial matter: how a piece of academic work should be evaluated isn't as important as all that. But in life we're chronically involved in a crisis of evaluation. Here it's not a matter of evaluating limited achievements, but of evaluating life as a whole.

Such fundamental crises don't just arise over the really major questions, for example, whether it will be possible to prevent wars. After all, what is peace? In war, human wickedness is organized collectively towards one great goal. In peace it sets itself many small goals. The human tendency towards degeneration gets split up. Great crises turn into skirmishes which do limited damage. But even here people constantly amass arms, count batallions, stage psychological warfare, call for capitulation. You only have to imagine all these petty evils directed towards a goal, and you have a major war. Let's not forget that the people who make war are the same as those who organize peace.

Once that dawns on us, and we are no longer so surprised at the everyday war, then we are in great danger of taking two steps towards the abyss.

The first step is to give way to contempt for human beings, to give human beings a notoriously bad press – indeed to expect them to behave without peace and reconciliation.

The second step into the abyss is for it to dawn on us that we are no better than the rest, that we have within ourselves the germ of all the lesser and greater evils that we observe in others. Then universal contempt for others becomes contempt for ourselves, which poisons and destroys life.

That is what I call the great crisis in evaluating life.

What is now happening in the lesser crisis of evaluating work – the sudden recollection of someone who made a mark on us – happens to Christians in the face of this great crisis of evaluation: when our courage to live and die is in crisis, then the image of Jesus emerges in us. He is the teacher of all of us. He shakes his head when we begin to despise other people and ourselves. He lives in our hearts. When his picture takes hold of us, we have passed from life to death. Then we are a living community.

But are we a living community in this sense? Are we better than the community of Sardis? It, too, was told, 'You have a reputation for being alive, but you are dead.' But then follows the admonition, 'Wake up! Strengthen what remains and is about to die!' Yet how are we to strengthen what is about to die? In my experience, abstract words are of little use here. One needs the power of a poet to bring alive this courage to live and die. To attempt that I've chosen two different genres. First I shall recount a little myth, a story about God. I've made it up, but it's true.

Imagine that we aren't yet born. Our souls are together in heaven. God distributes roles on earth. He comes to me, too, and makes me various offers. But I say to the first, 'I don't want that role: I want to live a long time and not die so early.' I say to the next, 'I don't want that role: what could I do in the world if I had no power and no means?' And to the third I say, 'That's not my role either. I couldn't bear being despised.' And so it goes on. After I've tried the patience of the Most High sorely, he finally says: 'Perhaps it will be easier for you if I tell you what role I've chosen for myself. I shall live for about thirty years. I shall have no house, no family, no income. I shall be despised by my relatives. My friends will leave me in the lurch. In the end I shall be executed as a criminal.' I say, 'But, Lord, what can you do in such a role? How can you bring creation nearer to its goal? How can you influence people?' And he says to me, 'I'll show you that I can do more in this role than in any other. I'll convince people by it that I love them. I'll convince them that they are worth something in the smallest role, and can change the world.' I object, 'But wouldn't it be better for you to change the whole creation so that it's no longer the hell that it sometimes seems to be?' And he says, 'There is no hell. But I will descend into what you call hell. My love for men and women and for creation will be stronger than this hell.'

Let's leave the mythological imagery aside. Christian courage to live and die is based on an unconditional 'Yes' to life – not only to its good side as we continually experience it, but also to its dark side, even to martyrdom, should that be required of us.

Now for a second attempt. It occurs in the Revelation of John. It, too, is a poem, a large-scale poem. It shows in visionary imagery how the world threatens to fall apart, how it becomes hell, because human beings transgress the boundary between God and humankind. But in all this hellish terror there is one firm point, Jesus. He is depicted as the lamb who opens the seals of the book in which the chaotic events are contained. He comes like the thief who beyond all order confronts human beings with the decision whether they are ready to suffer for the truth or not. He appears as the chief secretary in heaven, who enters men and women in the book of life. He is both these at the same time: the thief who disrupts all order and the secretary who in the last instance is responsible for the ordering of human destinies.

These images and visions cannot be held to be true or false. They are poems. They don't say much about the external world. Rather, they seek to change our perception of the external world. The visions of the Revelation of John assure us that even if the world becomes chaotic and the human tendency towards degeneration makes it hell, we may still have unconditional courage to live and die. For this courage is no naive original courage. It is shaped by the figure of Christ. It has been crucified and buried, and has risen again with him.

So what is a living community? A living community is one which emanates such courage, even in peaceful times, that it is equipped for the time of testing. This can come at any time, like a thief in the night. Then it will emerge whether our courage to live is also courage to die.

But this courage for martyrdom is Christian courage only if it is not the consequence of contempt for life but the consequence of an unconditional yes to life, a sign of the boundless love of God with which we then go on to love ourselves and others, even when we are horrified at the human tendency towards degeneration.

If we sense in our hearts this love of God for all creatures, so that our yes to life also becomes part of this love, we shall experience in living and dying that blessing with which I would like to end: may the peace of God which passes all our understanding keep our hearts and minds in Jesus Christ. Amen.

The Need for Repentance
On the inevitability of human 'lukewarmness'

(Revelation 3.14-22)

To the angel of the church in Laodicea write: 'These are the words of the Amen, the faithful and true witness, the ruler of God's creation. I know your deeds, that you are neither cold nor hot. I wish you were either one or the other. So because you are lukewarm – neither hot nor cold – I am about to spit you out of my mouth. You say, "I am rich; I have acquired wealth and do not need a thing." But you do not realize that you are wretched, pitiful, poor, blind and naked. I counsel you to buy from me gold refined in the fire, so that you can become rich; and white clothes to wear, so that you can cover your shameful nakedness; and salve to put on your eyes, so that you can see. Those whom I love I rebuke and discipline. So be earnest, and repent. Here I am! I stand at the door and knock. If anyone hears my voice and opens the door, I will come in and eat with him, and he with me. To him who overcomes, I will give the right to sit with me on my throne, just as I overcame and sat down with my Father on his throne. He who has an ear, let him hear what the Spirit says to the churches.'

Ever since I became a college teacher, I've kept hearing a 'message' to repent reminiscent of the message of the Revelation of John to the church in Laodicea. It's sent by students and addressed to 'the professors'. If I may fuse the words of the Apocalypse with those of the students, this message runs: 'We know your commitment. You're neither hot nor cold. You're lukewarm, academically calm and thoughtful. If only you were really reactionary or rebellious (as some of you are reputed to be)! But as it is, you're neither hot nor cold, and we can't stand you. Because you've become rich, because you've successfully become integrated into the higher echelons of our society, you've lost sensitivity to the suffering of others, to the great tasks of the world: the fight against hunger, war, oppression.

175

You think only of your books and research, building your homes and your own little world. You'd do better to get out into the front line. Listen to some home truths. You're blind. Change the way you act. Don't think that we don't love you. The reason why we're criticizing you so vigorously is because we expect something of you, especially you professors of theology. You couldn't resist being academic figures like all the rest. You've more obligations to God than anyone else. Look, we're standing at the door and knocking: we would very much like to come in and share your lives, eat and drink together. Perhaps then you wouldn't sit so firmly on your professorial chairs, but on chairs nearer to us.'

That's the kind of message I keep getting through various channels. Today is a day of penitence and prayer – certainly an occasion for professors of theology to take a look at themselves. Isn't there truth in this message? Doesn't the message of those prophets who berate us for our lukewarmness hit the target?

Let me respond on three points.

1. I would like to offer some defence of human lukewarmness.

2. I would like to make clear why I think that repentance – including radical repentance and a change of attitude – is necessary.

3. I would like to ask on what criteria we have to say, 'Here a radical change of attitude, conversion, is necessary.'

So first of all an apologia for human lukewarmness. Let me say quite openly: I can't stand some prophets of the great Either-Or. If only they had the intellectual charm, the tact and the vulnerability with which Kierkegaard posed us the Either-Or of Christian faith! But tact is not a characteristic of those moral prophets who say, 'Swine or not swine, that's the question.' They've yet to understand that in human life there are intermediate stages between non-swine and swine.

I can't stand the guardians of piety who press one into a corner and demand, 'Do you believe in Jesus Christ the Son of God?', in a tone which already makes it clear that you will be reckoned with the goats on the Day of Judgment.

I have reservations about those prophets of culture who assure us that all the evil in the world derives from the fact that human beings have too little skin contact – from infancy to old age – and that is why they make war so much. They're not stroked enough. I'm all for stroking. It's good. But it doesn't do away with wars.

And I've yet to mention the most important reason for my antipathy to these Either-Or prophets. The decisive reason is that those who make their standpoint a 'Here I stand' question in discussions remove it from democratic compromise. I'm convinced that life in our churches, in the university, in society, will work only if we can discuss the majority of themes quietly, without being completely hot or completely cold. Those who measure everything by the criterion of the absolute will see this only as reprehensible lukewarmness. But we are asked to show such lukewarmness. Without it life would become hell – it would become all too hot, indeed hellishly hot.

Now to the second point: today is a day of penitence and prayer, and you rightly expect something other than a commendation of human lukewarmness. Penitence is a change of behaviour – a radical change of behaviour. It is necessary, bitterly necessary. I am deeply convinced of this (despite all my love of human lukewarmness) – as a human being, as a scholar and as a Christian.

I am convinced as a human being that repentance is necessary. Animals cannot repent. Animals have fixed behavioural programmes. If environmental conditions change, they are dependent on chance mutations for adapting to the changes. Variants which do not adapt are doomed to extinction. By contrast, human beings deliberately correct their behaviour. They can register that the conditions within which they live have changed and that they could not survive without changing their behaviour. They can allow behavioural patterns to die out so that they themselves do not die out: for example, the behaviour pattern of that ethnocentric militarism which was appropriate for coping with mailed fist, sword and shield, but which in a world of nuclear and chemical weapons must lead to catastrophe. Here repentance is necessary. Here repentance and a change of behaviour is our only chance of life. Today there will be more talk about that in this church in the context of Peace Week. The day of penitence and prayer is a good starting point.

I am convinced as a scholar that repentance is necessary. Scholarship and science consist in a capacity to correct errors, safeguarded by sound method. Scholarship and science represent a constant intellectual repentance, a change of behaviour in the sphere of cognitive attitudes. That is what makes sciences humane: the scholar eliminates hypotheses instead of human beings. Granted, scientific thought does not guarantee humanity. But contempt for scholarship and science, i.e. contempt for a capacity to correct errors safe-guarded by sound method, is a guaranteed way to inhumanity.

At the beginning I quoted that 'message' which often comes to me from the students. There are often signs of a terrifying alienation between students and teachers. I don't believe that this alienation can effectively be overcome by more personal contacts. I can meet only a small number of students personally. There are too many of them. What seems to me decisive is that teachers and students should once again acquire greater respect for their common task. We need to recognize the magnitude of scholarship and science. It is the methodical attempt to kill off hypotheses so that human beings do not have to die. Our society is dependent for its survival on our disseminating this basic scientific attitude – and not just among professors and doctoral students. It is also important for students with modest intellectual resources to have some awareness of this – indeed everyone should have some awareness of this spirit. If our self-respect is based on respect for a common cause, then we shall have better human relationships – even in over-filled lecture rooms and seminars which are all too large.

Now finally to the most important thing: for Christians and Jews (I can't think of anything to divide us here) change of behaviour, repentance and penance are a divine demand. God does not want the sinner to die, but to repent and live (Ezek.33.11). This demand for repentance is connected with biblical belief in God, belief in the one and only God, who governs all reality from the remotest galaxies to the smallest particles. This faith is formulated in the Bible as a sharp alternative: from Elijah to the Revelation of John the question is, 'God or the idols?' Others might tell themselves that the many gods are only different manifestations of the one Godhead and therefore could simply add together different modes of behaviour, just as the corresponding gods were 'added' to a family of gods. But in the Bible the message is that the one God is the stark alternative to all idols. To turn to God is to renounce all modes of behaviour which are connected with the idols. To turn to this God is repentance, a change of attitude. And vice versa, where turning to this God does not involve repentance, we do not have to do with God, but with an idol. The Bible is the great textbook in which we human beings first spelled out the need for a radical change of attitude – and even now we haven't fully learned the lesson.

This belief in the one God who calls for repentance sheds light on changes of behaviour in life and science; in the light of faith I can interpret the demands for a change in behaviour which we come across everywhere when confronted with this one God.

The whole of human life, indeed life generally, from the smallest cells to the most complicated neural structures, then seems to us to be an infinite process of trial and error aimed at according with this one God – a process which takes place unconsciously in living beings (and even in us is only partly conscious), in which we participate with our whole body, all our nerves and our whole behaviour and thought. But we have an opportunity to make this process conscious. We can consciously lead our life as a response to God's demand. We can understand our life as a hypothesis aimed at according with God, a hypothesis which calls for constant correction, constant repentance, constant change of behaviour.

But where should this repentance lead us? That brings us to my third point: are there criteria by which to judge when the radical demand for a change of behaviour is necessary – just as it is regarded as unconditionally necessary in the biblical demand for change?

The letter to the church in Laodicea leaves obscure what the specific requirements are. Only from the overall context of Revelation can we recognize a problem: the emperor cult. Revelation is about a remarkable forced imposition of this cult in the time of Domitian, who was the first to let himself be addressed as 'Lord and God'. It is about the age-old problem of god or idols. Wouldn't that be a criterion? Wherever human beings put themselves in the place of God is the point of decision. At that point there is only an Either-Or.

But God and the idols have become anonymous today. No institution divinizes itself in so clearly recognizable a way as that emperor Domitian who entitled himself *dominus et deus*. There the dividing lines were clear. Nevertheless, we know clearly today where we run the risk of overstepping our limits. Human beings overstep their limits where they declare individual groups or whole peoples second-class, whether in order to exploit them economically, as in South Africa, or to exterminate them, as in National Socialist Germany. There can be no compromise with racism.

Human beings overstep their limits where states define the conditions in which the destruction of our culture by modern weapons would be justified. Anyone who includes that in strategic planning is usurping the role of God. There can be no compromise with this militarism.

The state oversteps its limits where it wants to put the conscience under public control. It must respect areas in which it cannot intervene with regulations and laws, decrees and oaths. There can be no compromise with totalitarianism, of no matter what stamp. In my view, all that is evident to Christian people. Or to put it more tentatively: it is evident to me. The problem begins when conclusions are made specific. We must respect the fact that here Christians differ. Not signing petitions against apartheid does not necessarily make one a racist. Doubting whether any peace strategy can be successful does not make one a militarist. Refusal to reject any form of examination of applicants for public service does not make one a fascist. Anyone who lightly undertakes a heresy hunt against others on these points destroys the presuppositions for the necessary discussion of such questions.

For there is another way in which human beings overstep their limits which I haven't yet mentioned: human beings usurp the role of the last judge when they think that they can divide one another all too precisely into children of light and children of darkness.

So this is our situation – and there is no point in brushing it aside with smart slogans: we clearly suspect that we may possibly be doing fundamental things wrong, and if we don't correct them they could lead us into the abyss. We have a fairly good idea where we may be doing these things wrong, but we don't know precisely what is asked of us. Repentance, conversion, a change of attitude, are necessary – but in what direction?

For many people that is a cause for resignation and pessimism. So let me end with an illustration.

Our situation is that of a school class. God is like a mathematics teacher who has set the pupils a difficult problem and then leaves the classroom. It's a remarkable class: teachers and beginners are sitting side by side in it. All keep calculating and calculating, but the problem seems insoluble. Some don't trust the teacher and say, 'The problem's insoluble. The teacher's played a dirty trick on us.' Even some professors hold this view. Gradually it dawns on others that they can't solve the problem with the formulae they know. They have to develop new ones, bring about a 'conversion' in their intellectual strategies. This group also includes some beginners who can't believe that there could be such a thing as a malicious teacher. They hold firm to their belief: 'Our teacher has set us a problem. He's confident that we shall solve it. He has more confidence in us than we have in ourselves. He's encouraging us to adopt a new approach, to turn from our previous ways.' So we, too, should say, 'God is complicated, but not malicious.' God has set us a difficult problem, but in principle it is not insoluble.

This doesn't just apply to the solving of great problems. I know that many people despair of ever solving their personal problems. They begin to become mistrustful of those who have created these problems for them: they convince themselves that they have been set an insoluble task – perhaps even a malicious task. And perhaps it really is insoluble unless we help them.

But what if whole people, whole societies, talk themselves into such mistrust? It's the start of giving up.

That makes it all the more important for us – for each individual, but also for all of us together as members of our society – to hear the good news of repentance: God gives us the chance to change our behaviour. God has confidence in us even when we have no confidence in ourselves. God is more confident in us than our lack of courage would have it.

So may the peace of God, which passes all our understanding, keep your hearts and minds in Christ Jesus. Amen.

Notes

Cain and Abel

This sermon was preached on 15 May 1988 at the Peterskirche in Heidelberg. The reappraisal of the case of 'Cain' has a long history. In terms of cultural history his descendants were already depicted in the Old Testament as representatives of progress: according to Gen.4.17-22 they built the first city, lived in tents, and were musicians and skilled smiths. In early Christianity Cain was reappraised in some small heretical groups. Irenaeus reports the existence of the 'Cainites' (*Adversus haereses* I, 31,1-2); they are said to have seen Cain, Esau and the traitor Judas as representatives of the true God, who were fought against by the subordinate creator god (the God of the Old Testament). In modern times, in his great novel *East of Eden* (1952), Steinbeck presented the story of Cain and Abel as a drama of human freedom and guilt. For him, the understanding of Gen.4.7 as a promise plays a major part: 'You will become master over sin.'

Jacob and Esau

This sermon was preached on 10 April 1981 at the Peterskirche in Heidelberg, as one of a series on 'Peace'. The declaration of German professors mentioned in it is the 'Call by German Churchmen and Professors to Evangelical Christians Abroad', made at the end of August 1914, and so castigated by Karl Barth. Its signatories included A.Deissmann, A.von Harnack, W.Herrmann, F.Loofs, G.Wobbermin and also the philosophers Rudolf Eucken and Wilhelm Wundt. The sermon was written under the impact of the relapse into the Cold War marked by the invasion of Afghanistan by Soviet troops (1979) and the Polish crisis (1980/1981). At that time supporters of the Reagan administration, which had been in power since 1981, had been arguing that we were not in a post-war but a pre-war situation: in the long term Eastern and Western social systems could not co-exist. But there was also a relapse into the Cold War even within West Germany: since my return from Denmark in 1980 I had had the impression that the alienation between intellectual and official culture had increased under the impact of a conservative trend.

The Obstinate Prophecy

This sermon was preached on 24 December 1987 at the Christmas Eve service in the Peterskirche in Heidelberg; it was published for the first time in *Neue Stimme 1988*, 16-18, under the title 'The Holy Family in 1988 [sic!]'. During the year, on 25 May, there had been a controversial census in West Germany. It was boycotted by only a few groups, but many citizens were reluctant to be involved in it – especially as previous drafts of the law enacting it had been declared unconstitutional, since it grossly abused the right of citizens to control available information about themselves. In Schleswig-Holstein Prime Minister Uwe Barschel, of the Christian Democrats, had been forced to resign after disclosures of Machiavellian procedures during an election campaign. To hush up his misdeeds he had forced various colleagues and secretaries to commit perjury and had given his 'word of honour' to the German public at a press conference that the accusations against him were unfounded. All proved justified, and he committed suicide in Geneva on 11 October 1987. During this year several European countries, including West Germany, tightened up laws about immigrants and those seeking asylum. Nevertheless, before the end of the year there were decisive moves in a positive direction. For the first time the USSR and USA signed an agreement on the removal of land-based medium-range missiles, the INF treaty of 8 December 1987. Only a few people had thought this possible. The Prime Minister of Bavaria at that time, Josef Strauss, was so confident that the negotiations would fail that he publicly vowed that he would make a pilgrimage to Altötting on foot and light a candle to the image of the Virgin Mary if there was agreement. The then Minister of Defence, Manfred Wörner, went even further, and promised that he would crawl on his knees from Stuttgart to Bonn if a single missile was dismantled.

Letters to Exiles

This sermon was preached on 23 October 1988 at the service for the beginning of the semester held in the Peterskirche in Heidelberg. It was first published under the title, 'You are to build houses', in *Neue Stimme 1989*, 17-20. The reason for the polemic against post-modern astrology is that shortly beforehand I had come across an article by a professor of psychology at a well known German university which in all seriousness set out to demonstrate statistically the influence of constellations of planets on human destinies. The assessment of such considerations expressed in the sermon by the prophet Jeremiah is identical with my own.

Jesus as Exorcist

This sermon was preached on 8 November 1981 at the Peterskirche in Heidelberg. The controversy over labelling deviant behaviour as 'sickness' is described in H.Keupp (ed.), *Der Krankheitsmythos in der Psychopathologie*, Munich, Berlin and Vienna 1972. I found the interpretation of 'seeing ghosts' as a relic of an archaic proneness to anxiety in H.Ditfurth, *Der Geist fiel nicht von Himmel. Die Evolution unseres Bewusstseins*, Hamburg 1976, 167-9. He quotes (without a reference) a saying by K.Lorenz, 'Ghosts are projections of nocturnal predators'.

Dealing with Religious Prejudices

This sermon was preached on 8 June 1986 at the Peterskirche in Heidelberg and first published in *Neue Stimme 1986*, 23-5. I have described the historical background to Mark 7.24-30 and Matt.15.21-28 in *Lokalkolorit und Zeitgeschichte in den Evangelien*, Fribourg and Göttingen 1989, 63-85. In order to avoid misunderstanding I should stress that any religious conviction can become a prejudice if it contributes to rejecting help. So a particular religious conviction is not yet a prejudice. I should explain two allusions in the sermon. The people that brought about a non-violent revolution are the Filippinos. In 1984 the Philippine dictator Marcos had declared himself victor in the 14 May parliamentary elections, in which the vote had been manipulated. Non-violent unrest throughout the country led to his flight on 25 February 1985. In mentioning the 'harassment by some Congregations of Faith' of Third World theologians I had in mind the proceedings taken by the Roman Congregation of Faith under the German Cardinal Ratzinger against Leonardo Boff. The occasion for this was his book *Church: Charism and Power* (1981), Crossroad Publishing Company, New York and SCM Press, London 1985. On 3 April 1984 the Sacred Congregation for the Faith reacted with the document *Instructions on Some Aspects of the Theology of Liberation*, in which liberation theology was repudiated for its Marxist and evolutionary ideology with its incitement to violence. This work appeared a few days before the beginning of a 'hearing' of Boff before the Congregation of Faith and was publicly understood as condemnation in advance. The details of the hearing were not published, but Boff committed himself not to make public statements. On 8 May 1985 he was condemned to a 'silence in publishing', which prevented him from making further contributions to liberation theology. The ban was lifted on 2 April 1986. Perhaps it was even a small miracle that the Roman Curia changed its mind on some points.

The Sign Language of Baptism

This is an address before baptism and a sermon after it, given at St Peter's Church, Copenhagen, in summer 1979.

Help as a Representation of God

A meditation at the Wednesday morning service at the Peterskirche in Heidelberg on 28 June 1989. On 4 June 1989 the student demonstrations for a renewal of democracy in Tienanmen Square, 'The Place of Heavenly Peace', had been brought to a bloody end. In the following weeks many student leaders were condemned at show trials and executed. The hasidic stories of the good denial of God and of Rabbi Sussya come from M.Buber, *Tales of the Hasidim*; an abbreviated version of the German text was published by Thames and Hudson in 1956.

The Open Door

The Proclamation to Mary

A meditation at the Wednesday morning service at the Peterskirche in Heidelberg on 17 December 1986. The myth of the fall of the angels is widespread in apocalyptic literature (cf. Ethiopian Enoch 6-16).

The Our Father

A meditation at the Wednesday morning service at the Peterskirche in Heidelberg on 15 July 1987.

On Changing Human Beings and the World

A Bible study at the Berlin Kirchentag on 9 June 1989. The exegesis of the two parables of the fig tree was inspired by the work of Petra von Gemünden, *Vegetationsmetaphorik im Neuen Testament und seiner Umwelt. Eine Bildfelduntersuchung*, Heidelberg Dissertation 1989, on which I wrote an assessment while preparing the Bible study. For the thoughts about evolution sketched out at the end, see my book *Biblical Faith*, SCM Press and Fortress Press 1985.

The Open Door to Life

This sermon was preached on 22 November 1985 at the Peterskirche in Heidelberg. The fortieth anniversary of the founding of the German Democratic Republic on 7 October and an unusually large wave of refugees had sparked off an increasing number of demonstrations in favour of a democratization of the DDR. On 18 October the General Secretary, Erich Honecker, was dismissed – perhaps because he had argued that the 'unrest' should be put down by force. That is not certain. All we know is that hospitals in Leipzig, the centre of the demonstrations, were prepared for a bloody conflict between security forces and demonstrators. On 9 November the frontier within Germany was opened up again – and there were expectations that the Brandenburg Gate would also be reopned (which happened on 23 December). I have drastically abridged Franz Kafka's famous parable of the doorkeeper.

The Lost Sheep

This sermon was preached on 23 June 1985 at the Peterskirche in Heidelberg. The small sympathetic country mentioned in it, which does not want to lose any of its five million inhabitants and therefore introduced what Germans would consider extraordinary speed limits – i.e. 60 mph on autobahns – is Denmark. The sermon alludes to some scandals of 1984/5. The Flick scandal showed that our major industry systematically 'smeared' the Bonn politicians for its own ends. A questionable tax exemption of 800 million DM which benefited the Flick concerns coincided with substantial contributions by this business to the German political parties, especially to the Democrats, who appointed the economics ministers responsible for approving plans, Friedrichs and Lambsdorf. Proceedings against both ministers and against Herr von Brauchitsch of Flick were therefore begun on 29 August 1985. The list of political contributions from Flick contained the names of almost all the prominent politicians. However, the charge of corruption or attempted corruption could not be proved. The accused were therefore found guilty only of withholding tax. In the course of the proceedings Rainer Barzel, at the time Bundestag President, was shown to have had a so-called 'advisory position' with Flick. As a result, on 25 October 1984 he had to resign all offices.

For many people, the scandal over the Berlin battery factory Sonnenschein in summer 1984 showed that some branches of industry recklessly pollute the environment. Neither the legal system nor the authorities, which were themselves implicated in the scandal through lack of control and easygoing permissions, seemed to have been able to provide effective safeguards in the interest of those people living near the factory whose health had been endangered. A nice touch was that the factory belonged to Herr Schwarz-Schilling, who was minister of the postal system at the time. In the face of such scandal and intrigue the rapid resignation of the government spokesman Peter Boenisch on 14 June 1985 came a pleasant surprise. He resigned over irregularities in payment of tax, explaining that any citizen might have difficulties with the tax office, but not the government spokesman.

Believing and Thanking

This sermon was preached on 4 September 1988 at the Peterskirche in Heidelberg. A week earlier, on 28 August, a jet fighter had crashed into a crowd of spectators during an air display at Ramstein. While the service was being held, many of the seriously injured were still in hospital with little hope of survival. All in all seventy people perished. The Gladbeck hostage drama also took place at this time (on 16 August). After a bank raid two heavily-armed criminals took a large number of hostages and were pursued all over Germany. They killed two of them, an Italian boy and a young German woman. A policeman was also killed in the chase. W.Heisenberg has expressed his views on religion in his 1952 essay 'Positivismus, Metaphysik und Religion', in *Der Teil und das Ganze*, Munich 1973, 241-55. For an English text see *Physics and Beyond*, Allen and Unwin 1971, 215f. Here he describes the experience of central order as a kind of encounter with a 'Thou'. I owe the parable of the Alpine landscape to Dr K.Kakuschke (see my *On Having a Critical Faith*, SCM Press and Fortress Press 1979, 25f.).

Where is God?

This sermon was preached on 9 November 1986 in the village church of Gondelsheim. A large number of the professors in the Heidelberg theological faculty were preaching in local village churches in the district of

Bretten at that time, as part of the jubilee of Heidelberg University. The real aim was to win trust for university theology. This particular district had informed the authorities of the Baden Landeskirche of its anxiety that the professors of theology in Heidelberg were not being faithful to the Bible. So the sermon sought to gain understanding for scholarly interpretation of biblical texts. The conversation with members of the congregation after the service was a friendly one. The two rabbinic anecdotes come from M. Buber, *Tales of the Hasidim*, abbreviated edition, Thames and Hudson 1956.

Human Beings as God's Capital

This sermon was preached at Pentecost, 14 May 1989, at the Peterskirche in Heidelberg. H.Gülzow, *Christentum und Sklaverei in den ersten drei Jahrhunderten*, Bonn 1969, 146-73, has given an attractive historical-critical analysis of the career of Callistus; this sermon is based on his findings. There is further information on Callistus in S.G.Hall, 'Calixtus I (Bischof von Rom, reg.218-222)', *Theologische Realenzyklopädie* 7, 1981, 559-63.

Doubting Thomas

This sermon was preached on 10 April 1988, at the Peterskirche in Heidelberg.

The Restlessness of the Spirit

This sermon was preached at Pentecost, 22 May 1983, at the Peterskirche in Heidelberg. The story of the staplers is a free variation on the 'Story of the Hammer' in P.Watzlawick, *Anleitung zum Unglücklichsein*, Munich and Zurich 1983, 37f.

Science as the Art of Gardening

This sermon was preached on 6 May 1984 at the Peterskirche in Heidelberg, at the service for the beginning of the semester. It quotes an aphorism of G.C.Lichtenberg, *Werke* (ed.P.Plett), Hamburg 1967, 130: 'The fact that sermons are preached in churches does not do away with the need for lightning conductors on them.' The famous parable of the non-existent gardener comes from Antony Flew, in Antony Flew and Alasdair MacIntyre (eds.) *New Essays in Philosophical Theology*, SCM Press and Macmillan Co., 1955, 96ff. The description of human beings as gypsies of the universe comes from J.Monod, *Chance and Necessity*, Collins and Harper and Row 1972, 160: 'Man must at last wake out of his millenary dream and discover his total solitude, his fundamental isolation. He must realize that, like a gypsy, he lives on the boundary of an alien world; a world that is deaf to his music, and as indifferent to his hopes as it is to his suffering or his crimes.'

The Need for Repentance

Unknowing Hope

This sermon was given in Danish during the 1979 winter semester in Trinity Church, Copenhagen, at a student service. Only during 1979 had everyone become aware of the full extent of the genocide in Cambodia. After the end of the second Vietnam war (1964-1975) the Khmer Rouge had set up a regime of terror under Pol Pot to which between one and a half and two and a half million people fell victim. The victims were soldiers and members of the Lon Nol regime, supportes of Sihanouk, and independents. Intellectuals in particular were affected: eighty per cent of them were killed, and ninety per cent of teachers and doctors. Religious groups were persecuted: of 87,000 Buddhist monks, 82,000 were killed, and 500,000 out of 700,000 Muslims. The genocide was also directed against ethnic minorities: of originally 800,000 Chinese and Sino-Khmer only 30-40,000 survived. The Vietnamese invasion of Cambodia on 25 December 1978 contributed to the fall of the Pol Pot regime, but sparked off a catastrophic wave of refugees and a famine during 1979/80, not least because the Khmer Rouge adopted a scorched earth policy on their retreat to the frontier zones of Thailand. At that time shattering pictures of the refugees, of whom around half a million were encamped on both sides of the Cambodian borders, were going round the world.

Mourning at a Loss faced with Mass Graves

This sermon was preached on 16 November 1986, on the day of national mourning, at the Peterskirche in Heidelberg. Recollection of the Second World War was particularly vivid because of the commemoration of the fortieth anniversary of the end of the war in 1945. In an incredible gaffe, on 16 October 1986 Chancellor Kohl had compared Mikhail Gorbachev with Joseph Goebbels. Joseph Goebbels was born on 29 October 1887 in my home town of Rheydt (in the Rhineland), and like me went to the Hugo Junkers Gymnasium. Anecdotes about him as a schoolboy were still current in Rheydt. He gained his doctorate at Heidelberg University in 1922 with a thesis on 'Wilhelm von Schütz as Dramatist. A Contribution to the History of the Drama of the Romantic School'. Various quotations in the sermon come from E.Raiser, H.Lenhard and B.Homeyer (eds.), *Brücken der Verständigung. Für eine neues Verhältnis zur Sowjetunion*, Gütersloh 1986. The story of the German woman crane driver and the Russian girl is on pp.164-6. The person mentioned in the sermon who served in the war is my colleague H.E.Tödt. Cf. his contribution 'Deutsche Schuld im Krieg gegen die Sowjetunion 1941-1945' in the same book, 49-60:52. The claim that we have learned the 'lesson of history' is constantly made in the speeches by Chancellor Helmut Kohl.

Preparation for the Journey into an Unknown Land

This sermon was preached on 19 March 1986 at the Peterskirche in Heidelberg. The letter from Klaus Bonhoeffer to his daughter Cornelia appears in E.and R.Bethge (eds.), *Letzte Briefe im Widerstand: aus dem Kreis der Familie Bonhoeffer*, Munich 1984, 49f. The anecdote about the old farmer comes from Wilhelm von Scholz, *Das Buch des Lachens*, Munich 1944, 234f., reprinted in L.Graf, U.Kabitz et al., *Die Blumen des Blinden*, Munich 1983, 114f.

The End of the Compulsion to Sacrifice

This sermon was preached on 19 March 1986 at the Peterskirche in Heidelberg. At that time there was a vigorous debate in the church as to whether out of consideration for those who were afraid of catching Aids the practice observed hitherto of having a eucharist once a month should be dropped and the bread should be dipped in the chalice to make it possible for the 'weak' to take part in the eucharist without anxiety. However, some people saw this as a step towards breaking solidarity with Aids victims and groups with special Aids risks. At this time politicians made remarks which raised fears of a revival of antisemitism. Thus the burgomaster of Korschenbroich, Freiherr Graf von Spee, had said that to balance his town's budget it would be necessary to kill a Jew (he wanted to indicate that there was no money). He resigned on 14 February 1986. A preliminary enquiry with a view to criminal proceeding on grounds of inciting racial hatred was dropped when he paid 9000 DM to the children's cancer clinic in Düsseldorf. At this time the Christian Socialist deputy Herr Fellner, in connection with compensation payments for victims of National Socialism, remarked that Jews always appeared when money jingled in German banks. But above all the discussion over the Fassbender play 'The Refuse, the City and Death', performed in November 1985, raised the question whether in the meantime antisemitic attitudes and prejudices had not also become weaker among intellectuals. The theory of sacrifice sketched out in the sermon appears in W.Burkert, *Homo necans. Interpretationen altgriechischer Opferriten und Mythen*, Berlin and New York 1972. Freud put forward his theory of the sacrificial death of Jesus and the eucharist in 'Totem and Taboo', *Collected Works* 13, Penguin Books 1985, 43-224. J.W.Goethe speaks of the joyful lust for murder in his poem 'Journey through the Harz in Winter'.

Criteria for a Living Faith

This sermon was preached on 11 December 1983 at the Peterskirche in Heidelberg. Autumn 1983 saw the controversies over the installation of missiles, which made some people think that the *status confessionis* might arise again for them sooner than they would have liked. The myth recounted in the sermon is inspired by J.Rawls, *A Theory of Justice*, Oxford University Press 1972, esp. 150ff.

The Need for Repentance

This sermon for a day of penitence and prayer was preached on 17 November 1982 at the Peterskirche in Heidelberg. That year the day fell in the middle of a 'Peace Week'. It is impossible to render in English the word-play in the phrase 'Swine or not swine', which of course relates to Hamlet's famous soliloquy. German has 'Sein oder nicht sein/Schwein oder nicht Schwein'. The remark that it is better to kill off hypotheses comes from Karl Popper, *Objective Knowledge. An Evolutionary Sketch*, Oxford University Press ²1979, 244, 247; on p.261 he puts it like this: 'Thus while animal knowledge and pre-scientific knowledge grows mainly through the elimination of those holding the unfit hypotheses, scientific criticism often makes our theories perish in our stead, eliminating our mistaken beliefs before such beliefs lead to our own elimination.'